COOKING
AHEAD

GOOD HOUSEKEEPING
STEP-BY-STEP COOKERY

COOKING AHEAD

Guild Publishing/Ebury Press
LONDON

Consultant editor: Jeni Wright
Editors: Veronica Sperling and Sonya Mills
Design: Mike Leaman
Illustrations: John Woodcock and Kate Simunek
Photography: Melvin Grey
Cookery: Susanna Tee, Maxine Clark, Janet Smith

Cover photograph: Pork with Cider and Coriander (page 36)
and Mango Mousse (page 74)

Filmset by Advanced Filmsetters (Glasgow) Ltd

Printed and bound in Italy by
New Interlitho, S.p.a., Milan

CONTENTS

COOKERY NOTES

Follow either metric or imperial measures for the recipes in this book as they are not inter-changeable. Sets of spoon measures are available in both metric and imperial size to give accurate measurement of small quantities. All spoon measures are level unless otherwise stated. When measuring milk we have used the exact conversion of 568 ml (1 pint).

* Size 4 eggs should be used except when otherwise stated.

† Granulated sugar is used un-less otherwise stated.

● Plain flour is used unless otherwise stated.

OVEN TEMPERATURE CHART

°C	°F	Gas mark
110	225	$\frac{1}{4}$
130	250	$\frac{1}{2}$
140	275	1
150	300	2
170	325	3
180	350	4
190	375	5
200	400	6
220	425	7
230	450	8
240	475	9

KEY TO SYMBOLS

$\boxed{1.00*}$ Indicates minimum preparation and cooking times in hours and minutes. They do not include prepared items in the list of ingredients; calculated times apply only to the method. An asterisk * indicates extra time should be allowed, so check the note below symbols.

⌂ Chef's hats indicate degree of difficulty of a recipe: no hat means it is straightforward; one hat slightly more complicated; two hats indicates that it is for more advanced cooks.

£ Indicates a recipe which is good value for money; £ £ indicates an expensive recipe. No £ sign indicates an inexpensive recipe.

✳ Indicates that a recipe will freeze. If there is no symbol, the recipe is unsuitable for freezing. An asterisk * indicates special freezer instructions so check the note immediately below the symbols.

$\boxed{309\ cals}$ Indicates calories per serving, including any sugges-tions (e.g. cream, to serve) given in the ingredients.

METRIC CONVERSION SCALE

LIQUID			SOLID		
Imperial	Exact conversion	Recommended ml	Imperial	Exact conversion	Recommended g
$\frac{1}{4}$ pint	142 ml	150 ml	1 oz	28.35 g	25 g
$\frac{1}{2}$ pint	284 ml	300 ml	2 oz	56.7 g	50 g
1 pint	568 ml	600 ml	4 oz	113.4 g	100 g
$1\frac{1}{2}$ pints	851 ml	900 ml	8 oz	226.8 g	225 g
$1\frac{3}{4}$ pints	992 ml	1 litre	12 oz	340.2 g	350 g
For quantities of $1\frac{3}{4}$ pints and over, litres and fractions of a litre have been used.			14 oz	397.0 g	400 g
			16 oz (1 lb)	453.6 g	450 g
			1 kilogram (kg) equals 2.2 lb.		

COOKING AHEAD

Cooking ahead is sensible and practical—but this doesn't mean that cook-ahead recipes need be uninspiring. In this book there are Soups and Starters, Main Meals, Vegetables and Salads, Desserts and Baking ideas. An exciting collection of recipes, all of which can be prepared and cooked hours, even days, ahead of time. This is the perfect book to help you make everyday meals with a minimum of effort, and to make entertaining as relaxed as possible.

In the recipe section of the book, every dish is photographed in colour, with step-by-step illustrations to guide you smoothly through the methods. Detailed instructions are provided on preparation and cooking in advance, plus separate sections on the final touches to make before serving—at-a-glance information that all busy cooks will find an absolute boon.

In the tinted pages at the end of the book, there's information to help you with cook-ahead meals, plus basic recipes which form a useful reference section. There's lots of detail on ingredients and equipment, menu planning, preserving and freezing—plus a special section for Christmas, one of the most important occasions in the year when cooking ahead really comes into its own.

Soups and Starters

When you're entertaining, it's best to get the first course made in advance, then you can concentrate all your efforts on last-minute things like vegetables and salads, which are best served absolutely fresh. In this chapter you will find soups and starters which can be made at least the day before required—so there should be no panics on the night!

TERRINE OF CHICKEN WITH WINE

2.30* £ | 289–362 cals

* plus 6 hours chilling

Serves 8–10

450 g (1 lb) boneless chicken breasts

175 g (6 oz) rindless back bacon

25 g (1 oz) butter

25 g (1 oz) flour

150 ml ($\frac{1}{4}$ pint) dry white wine

2 eggs

7.5 ml ($1\frac{1}{2}$ tsp) salt

freshly ground pepper

15 ml (1 tbsp) fresh rosemary, crushed; or 5 ml (1 tsp) dried

15 ml (1 tbsp) lemon juice

1 large garlic clove, skinned and crushed

450 g (1 lb) pork belly, minced

rosemary sprigs, to garnish

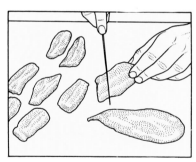

1 To prepare (2 hours): Remove the skin from the chicken and discard. Slice the breasts across into thin escalopes. Finely chop the bacon.

2 Melt the butter in a saucepan, add the flour and cook over low heat, stirring with a wooden spoon, for 2 minutes. Gradually blend in the wine, stirring after each addition to prevent lumps forming. Bring to the boil slowly, then simmer for 2–3 minutes, stirring.

3 Cool the sauce, then stir in the remaining ingredients except the chicken. Work well together.

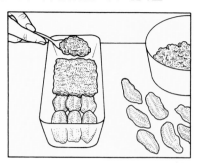

4 In a 1.4 litre ($2\frac{1}{2}$ pint) loaf tin, layer the chicken and the pork mixture, beginning with chicken and ending with pork.

5 Cover the dish with foil and place in a roasting tin. Pour in enough boiling water to come halfway up the sides of the dish.

6 Bake in the oven at 170°C (325°F) mark 3 for $1\frac{1}{2}$ hours. Remove from the roasting tin and cool slightly, then place heavy weights on top of the foil covering. Leave until cold, then chill in the refrigerator for at least 6 hours.

7 To serve (30 minutes): Remove the weights and foil covering from the terrine and drain off surplus juices. Leave at room-temperature for 30 minutes before serving. Garnish with rosemary sprigs.

Menu Suggestion

Serve this attractive layered pâté for a special occasion with hot bread rolls or French bread, and a bottle of Chablis.

FRENCH GARLIC PÂTÉ

2.50*	✳*	646 cals

* plus cooling and chilling after cooking; freeze after cooling in step 7

Serves 8

16 streaky bacon rashers
450 g (1 lb) pig's liver
450 g (1 lb) belly pork
225 g (8 oz) pork back fat (see box)
100 g (4 oz) crustless French bread (baguette)
4 garlic cloves, skinned
30 ml (2 tbsp) anchovy paste
45 ml (3 tbsp) brandy
10 ml (2 tsp) dried thyme
1.25 ml (¼ tsp) grated nutmeg
1 egg, beaten
salt and freshly ground pepper
sprigs of thyme, to garnish

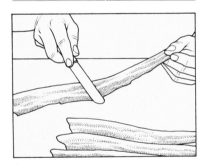

1 *To prepare* (2 hours 45 minutes): Cut the rinds off the bacon, then stretch the rashers with the flat of a knife blade.

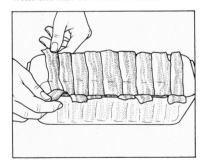

2 Use the bacon rashers to line the base and sides of a 1.4 litre (2½ pint) terrine or other ovenproof dish. Reserve enough rashers to cover the top.

3 Mince the liver, pork and fat with the bread and garlic (or work in a food processor if you prefer a pâté with a finer texture).

4 Turn the mixture into a bowl and add the remaining ingredients, with 2.5 ml (½ tsp) salt, and pepper to taste. Beat well to mix.

5 Spoon the mixture into the lined terrine, pressing it down well and levelling the surface. Cover the top of the pâté with the reserved bacon rashers, then cover the terrine loosely with foil.

6 Place the terrine in a roasting tin, then pour in enough boiling water to come halfway up the sides of the terrine. Bake in the oven at 170°C (325°F) mark 3 for 2 hours. Remove from the roasting tin and pour off any excess fat from the sides of the terrine.

7 Place heavy weights on top of the foil covering (to compress the pâté and make it easier to slice). Leave until cold, then chill for at least 24 hours (or up to 3 days).

8 *To serve* (5 minutes): Remove the weights and foil covering from the terrine. Loosen the pâté from the terrine by running a palette knife around the sides, then turn the pâté out on to a serving plate. Cut a few slices just before serving and garnish with thyme.

Menu Suggestion
This strongly flavoured pâté is best eaten with fresh crusty French bread and a full-bodied French red wine such as a Côte du Rhône.

FRENCH GARLIC PÂTÉ

Fat is essential in pâtés, to achieve moistness and richness. Pork back fat is used in French pâtés because it is smoother and firmer than other animal fats, and tastes good when served cold. Buy pork back fat from your butcher, telling him what you are going to use it for. He will generally sell it to you in the sheet, with the rind still attached, in which case chill it in the refrigerator to firm the fat before dealing with it. Place the sheet, rind side down, on a board or work surface. With a long sharp knife, work horizontally between the rind and the fat, lifting the fat up and away from the rind as you go along.

Discard the rind and chop the fat before mincing it with the liver and meat.

NUTTY CAMEMBERT PÂTÉ

0.20*	✳*	315–475 cals

* plus overnight chilling; freeze at the end of step 3

Serves 4–6

175 g (6 oz) soft ripe Camembert cheese

225 g (8 oz) full-fat soft cheese

2.5 ml (½ tsp) paprika

salt and freshly ground pepper

75 g (3 oz) finely chopped blanched almonds

extra paprika, to serve

4 Loosen the pâté from the dish by running a palette knife between the two. Turn the pâté out upside down on to a serving plate and peel off the lining paper. Chill overnight.

1 *To prepare* (15 minutes): Cut the rind off the Camembert, then work the cheese through a sieve into a bowl, or mix in a food processor until smooth.

2 Add the soft cheese, paprika and seasoning to taste. Beat vigorously with a wooden spoon to combine the ingredients well together.

3 Spoon the pâté into a greased and base-lined 300 ml (½ pint) dish or mould. Press down well and smooth the surface with the back of the spoon. Cover the dish and freeze for 1 hour.

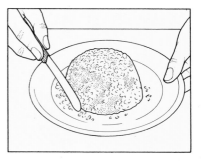

5 *To serve* (5 minutes): Sprinkle the nuts over the pâté, then press evenly over the top and around the sides with the palette knife. Sprinkle with paprika. Serve chilled.

Menu Suggestion

Cheese makes an unusual starter. Serve this creamy pâté with wholemeal toast, crispbreads or crackers.

SMOKED TROUT MOUSSE IN LEMON SHELLS

| 1.00* | ⊔ | ✳* | 197 cals |

* plus cooling, and chilling for at least 4 hours or overnight; freeze at the end of step 7

Serves 6

one 225 g (8 oz) smoked trout

6 large, even-sized lemons

300 ml (½ pint) milk

few slices each of onion and carrot

1 bay leaf

4–6 peppercorns

7.5 ml (1½ tsp) powdered gelatine

25 g (1 oz) butter or margarine

30 ml (2 tbsp) flour

15 ml (1 tbsp) creamed horseradish

90 ml (6 tbsp) double or whipping cream, whipped

1 egg white

salt and freshly ground pepper

chopped fresh parsley and sprigs of fresh herbs, to serve

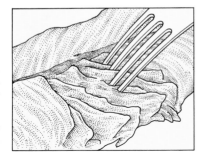

1 *To prepare* (55 minutes): Skin the trout and flake the flesh, discarding any bones. Cover and set aside.

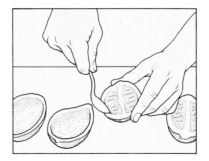

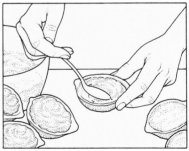

2 Cut the lemons in half lengthways and scoop out all the flesh and membranes with a sharp-edged teaspoon; reserve the shells. Measure 60 ml (4 tbsp) lemon juice, pour into a small heatproof bowl and reserve.

3 Bring the milk to the boil in a saucepan with the onion, carrot, bay leaf and peppercorns. Remove from the heat, cover and leave to infuse while preparing the mousse mixture.

4 Sprinkle the gelatine over the reserved measured lemon juice. Leave for 5 minutes until spongy, then stand the bowl in a pan of gently simmering water and heat until dissolved.

5 Melt the butter or margarine in a separate saucepan. Sprinkle in the flour and cook, stirring, for 1–2 minutes. Strain in the infused milk a little at a time, whisking vigorously until smooth. Simmer gently for 2 minutes, then turn into a bowl and stir in the liquid gelatine. Leave to cool.

6 Fold the flaked fish into the cold sauce with the horse-radish and whipped cream. Whisk the egg white until stiff, then fold in until evenly incorporated. Add seasoning, taking care not to add too much salt because the trout may be quite salty.

7 Spoon the mousse into the hollowed-out lemon shells, then chill in the refrigerator for at least 4 hours, or overnight if more convenient.

8 *To serve* (5 minutes): Arrange 2 lemon shells on each of 6 serving plates garnished with chopped parsley and a sprig of herbs. Serve chilled.

Menu Suggestion

These make elegant starters for a special dinner party. Follow with a main course of Casseroled Turkey in Red Wine (page 47) and Coffee Bavarian Cream (page 77) for dessert.

SMOKED TROUT MOUSSE IN LEMON SHELLS

If you are short of time and prefer not to serve this deliciously rich and creamy mousse in the lemon shells, it can be served simply in a large soufflé dish or individual ramekins. White china looks very pretty with the pale colour of the mousse, and you can garnish the tops with delicate 'butterflies' of sliced lemon. Cut a lemon into thin slices, then cut out opposite quarters, leaving the flesh intact in the middle. Press a small sprig of parsley or other herb into the centre.

STUFFED MUSHROOMS

| 1.05* | 🍲 | ✳* | 642 cals |

* plus 1 hour or overnight chilling;
freeze mushrooms and the dip
separately in step 6

Serves 4

30 ml (2 tbsp) olive oil

1 small onion, skinned and
chopped

2 garlic cloves, skinned and
crushed

396 g (14 oz) can tomatoes

5 ml (1 tsp) dried oregano

5 ml (1 tsp) dried basil

30 ml (2 tbsp) chopped fresh
parsley

1.25 ml ($\frac{1}{4}$ tsp) sugar

salt and freshly ground pepper

32 even-sized button mushrooms,
wiped

175 g (6 oz) unsalted butter,
softened

50 g (2 oz) can anchovies in olive
oil, drained and chopped

finely grated rind of 1 lemon

2 eggs, beaten

75 g (3 oz) dried breadcrumbs

vegetable oil for deep frying

1 To prepare (40 minutes): Make
the tomato dip. Heat the oil in
a saucepan, add the onion and half
the garlic and fry gently for 5
minutes until soft but not
coloured.

2 Add the tomatoes, dried herbs,
half the parsley, the sugar and
seasoning to taste. Bring to the
boil, stirring constantly with a
wooden spoon to break up the
tomatoes. Lower the heat and
simmer, covered, for 30 minutes,
stirring occasionally.

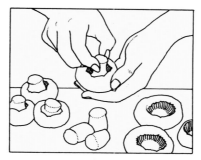

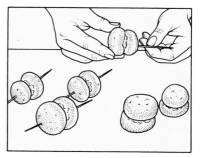

3 Meanwhile pull the stalks
carefully from the mushrooms
with your fingers. Chop the stalks
finely, then place in a bowl with
the butter, anchovies, lemon rind,
remaining garlic and parsley.
Beat the ingredients together
until well combined, then add
pepper to taste (do not add salt
because of the saltiness of the
anchovies).

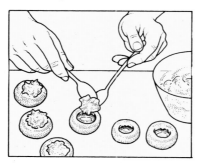

4 Spoon the butter mixture into
the cavities of each of the
mushrooms.

5 Sandwich the mushrooms
together in pairs and pierce
through the centre of each pair
with a wooden cocktail stick. Dip
the mushrooms in the beaten eggs,
then in the breadcrumbs until
evenly coated.

6 Chill in the refrigerator for 1
hour, or overnight if more
convenient. Remove the tomato
dip from the heat, leave to cool,
then chill in the refrigerator at the
same time as the mushrooms.

7 To serve (25 minutes): Work
the tomato dip in a blender or
food processor, then sieve to
remove the tomato seeds. Taste
and adjust seasoning, then pour
into a serving bowl or jug. Return
to the refrigerator while frying the
mushrooms.

8 Heat the oil in a deep frier to
190°C (375°F) and deep fry
the mushrooms in batches for
about 5 minutes until golden
brown and crisp on all sides.
Drain quickly on absorbent kitchen
paper, then remove the cocktail
sticks. Serve immediately, with
the chilled tomato dip handed
separately.

Menu Suggestion
This dinner party starter is so
substantial that it needs no
accompaniment other than chilled
dry white wine.

HADDOCK AND PRAWN GRATINÉE

| 0.50 | £ | 175 cals |

Serves 8

450 g (1 lb) haddock fillet, skinned

25 g (1 oz) butter

125 g (4 oz) onion, skinned and finely chopped

30 ml (2 tbsp) plain flour

300 ml ($\frac{1}{2}$ pint) milk

30 ml (2 tbsp) dry white wine

175 g (6 oz) frozen prawns, thawed

75 g (3 oz) Gruyère or mature Cheddar cheese, grated

salt and freshly ground pepper

chopped fresh parsley, to garnish

1 To prepare (20 minutes): Cut the haddock fillet into 12 small strips. Fold strips in half and place two each in 6 individual ramekin or gratin dishes.

2 Melt the butter in a saucepan, add the onion and fry gently until soft. Add the flour and cook over low heat, stirring with a wooden spoon, for 2 minutes. Remove the pan from the heat and gradually blend in the milk and wine, stirring after each addition to prevent lumps forming. Bring to the boil slowly, then simmer for 2–3 minutes, stirring.

3 Remove the sauce from the heat, add the prawns and 50 g (2 oz) of the cheese with seasoning to taste.

4 Spoon a little sauce into each ramekin, to cover the fish. Sprinkle the remaining cheese on top. Cool and chill in the refrigerator until required.

5 To serve (30 minutes): Bake in the oven at 190°C (375°F) mark 5 for 30 minutes. Serve immediately garnished with chopped parsley.

Menu Suggestion

Serve this hot, bubbling starter with French bread and chilled dry white wine.

HADDOCK AND PRAWN GRATINÉE

Haddock has a mild flavour and fairly firm texture, so is a good choice for this dinner party starter. A more expensive fish which can also be used is monkfish—now becoming available at most good fishmongers. Monkfish tastes similar to lobster and has very firm, meaty flesh, ideal for gratinée dishes such as this one, and for kebabs, casseroles and fish pies. For this recipe, buy monkfish fillets, then dice them rather than cutting them into strips.

STUFFED COD CRÊPES

1.40 | ▢ | £ | ✳ | 541 cals

Serves 6

175 g (6 oz) plain flour, plus 45 ml (3 tbsp)

50 g (2 oz) salted peanuts, very finely chopped

2 eggs

15 ml (1 tbsp) vegetable oil

450 ml (¾ pint) milk and water mixed

700 g (1½ lb) cod fillets

568 ml (1 pint) milk

50 g (2 oz) butter

125 g (4 oz) celery, chopped

5 ml (1 tsp) curry powder

salt and freshly ground pepper

75 ml (5 tbsp) single cream

50 g (2 oz) Cheddar cheese, grated

chopped fresh parsley, to garnish

1 *To prepare* (1 hour): Make the batter for the crêpes. Whisk 175 g (6 oz) flour, the chopped peanuts, eggs, oil and half the milk and water mixture until quite smooth. Whisk in the remaining liquid.

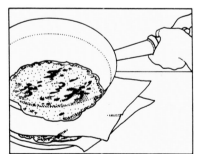

2 Make twelve 18.5 cm (7½ inch) crêpes in the usual way (see page 156). Keep covered.

3 Wash and dry the fish and place in a large sauté or deep frying pan with the milk. Cover and poach gently for about 12 minutes until the fish is quite tender and begins to flake. Strain off and reserve the liquid. Flake the fish, discarding skin and bone.

4 Melt the butter in a heavy-based saucepan, add the celery and curry powder and fry gently for 1 minute, stirring. Remove from the heat and stir in the remaining flour, reserved liquid from cooking the fish and seasoning to taste. Bring to the boil, stirring; simmer for 1 minute. Remove from the heat and fold in the cream and flaked fish.

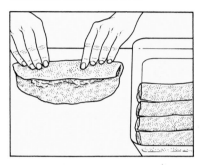

5 Divide the filling between the crêpes, roll up and place side by side in a single layer in a greased shallow ovenproof dish. Sprinkle the grated cheese over the top and cover loosely with foil. Chill in the refrigerator until required.

6 *To serve* (40 minutes): Bake in the oven at 180°C (350°F) mark 4 for about 40 minutes. Serve piping hot, sprinkled with chopped parsley.

Menu Suggestion
This is a substantial starter, which should be served on its own. Follow with a light main course such as Marinated Lamb Cutlets (page 30) and a fresh fruity salad for dessert.

CHILLED RATATOUILLE

| 0.45* | £ | ✳ | 142 cals |

* plus 30 minutes cooling and 4 hours chilling
Serves 6

1 large aubergine, about 350 g
   (12 oz) in weight
salt and freshly ground pepper
450 g (1 lb) courgettes
225 g (8 oz) trimmed leeks
450 g (1 lb) tomatoes
1 green pepper
60 ml (4 tbsp) vegetable oil
125 g (4 oz) button mushrooms,
   wiped
150 ml (¼ pint) chicken stock
30 ml (2 tbsp) tomato purée
15 ml (1 tbsp) chopped fresh
   rosemary, or 2.5 ml (½ tsp) dried

1 *To prepare* (40 minutes): Wipe the aubergine, discard the ends and cut the flesh into large fork-sized pieces.

2 Put the aubergine pieces in a colander or sieve, sprinkle liberally with salt and set aside to drain for 30 minutes.

3 Rinse under cold running water and pat dry with absorbent kitchen paper.

4 Wipe the courgettes and slice diagonally into 5 mm (¼ inch) thick pieces, discarding the ends.

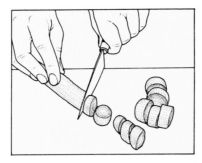

5 Cut the leeks across into similar sized pieces, discarding the root ends and any tough dark leaves. Wash, pushing the slices apart, and drain well.

6 Skin and quarter the tomatoes; push out the pips into a nylon sieve placed over a bowl. Reserve the tomato juice. Halve each tomato quarter lengthwise. Slice the pepper into narrow strips, discarding the seeds.

7 Heat the oil in a large sauté or frying pan. Add the aubergine and courgettes and fry over high heat for 2–3 minutes, turning frequently. Stir in the remaining vegetables with the chicken stock, tomato purée, reserved tomato juice, rosemary and seasoning to taste.

8 Bring the contents of the pan to the boil, cover and simmer for 8–10 minutes. The vegetables should be just tender with a hint of crispness, not mushy. Adjust the seasoning and pour out into a bowl to cool for 30 minutes. Chill well in the refrigerator for at least 4 hours.

9 *To serve* (5 minutes): Taste and adjust seasoning, then turn into a large serving bowl or individual dishes. Serve chilled.

Menu Suggestion
Serve for a dinner party starter with hot garlic bread. Marinated Lamb Cutlets (page 30) would make a good main course to follow, with Raspberry Almond Flan (page 67) for dessert.

CHILLED RATATOUILLE

Ratatouille is known more as a hot vegetable dish than as a chilled starter, yet in France it is often served cold, as part of a mixed hors d'oeuvre. French cooks use leftover ratatouille from the day before, which has chilled overnight in the refrigerator, to add colour and flavour to *hors d'oeuvre variés*. In fact, you will find that ratatouille always tastes better if it has been kept overnight before serving—even if you are serving it as a hot vegetable accompaniment (it goes particularly well with roast lamb or grilled lamb chops with rosemary).

Ratatouille originated in Provence, in the sunny south of France, where all the colourful summer vegetables grow in such profusion. There are literally hundreds of different versions, some of which are pungent with garlic and onions—two of the most prolific Provençal vegetables.

CREAM OF PARSLEY SOUP

| 0.55 | £ | ✳ | 125 cals |

Serves 8

225 g (8 oz) parsley

225 g (8 oz) onions, skinned

125 g (4 oz) celery, washed and trimmed

50 g (2 oz) butter or margarine

45 ml (3 tbsp) plain flour

2 litres (3½ pints) chicken stock, preferably jellied homemade (see page 154)

salt and freshly ground pepper

150 ml (¼ pint) single cream

parsley sprigs, to garnish

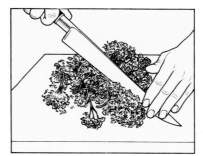

1 To prepare (45 minutes): Wash the parsley, drain and chop roughly. Slice the onions and celery.

2 Melt the fat in a large saucepan and add the parsley, onions and celery. Cover the pan and cook gently for about 10 minutes until the vegetables are quite soft. Shake the pan from time to time.

3 Stir in the flour until smooth, then mix in the stock. Add seasoning to taste and bring to the boil.

4 Cover the pan and simmer for 25–30 minutes. Cool a little, then purée in a blender or food processor. Leave to cool completely, then chill in the refrigerator until required.

5 To serve (10 minutes): Reheat until bubbling, taste and adjust seasoning and swirl in the cream. Serve immediately, garnished with the parsley.

Menu Suggestion

Serve this creamy soup in summer when there is plenty of fresh parsley in the garden. Hot French bread or garlic bread would make the perfect accompaniment.

CREAM OF PARSLEY SOUP

This soup can be made in next to no time if you have a food processor. Simply put the parsley, onions and celery in together and chop finely, then add the butter or margarine, flour and stock and work to a smooth purée. Transfer to a saucepan and bring to the boil, stirring constantly until thickened. Lower the heat and simmer as in the recipe. If you like, you can work the soup in the machine again before serving, for a really velvety smooth texture.

CURRIED PARSNIP AND ORANGE SOUP

0.55* £ ✱* 276 cals

* plus cooling and overnight standing;
freeze after blending in step 3

Serves 4

50 g (2 oz) butter or margarine

2 medium parsnips, peeled and
   diced

1 medium onion, skinned and
   chopped

1 garlic clove, skinned and crushed

5 ml (1 tsp) curry powder

5 ml (1 tsp) ground cumin

15 ml (1 tbsp) flour

1.1 litres (2 pints) chicken stock
   (see page 154)

finely grated rind and juice of 2
   large oranges

salt and freshly ground pepper

150 ml ($\frac{1}{4}$ pint) single cream,
   to serve

1 To prepare (45 minutes): Melt
the butter or margarine in a
large heavy-based saucepan. Add
the parsnips and onion, cover the
pan and fry gently for about 10
minutes until softened, shaking
the pan frequently.

2 Add the garlic and spices and
fry, uncovered, for 2 minutes,
stirring constantly to prevent
burning. Stir in the flour and cook
for a further 2 minutes, then pour
in the stock and the orange juice.
Bring to the boil, stirring, then
add seasoning to taste. Lower the
heat, cover and simmer for about
20 minutes until the parsnips are
tender.

3 Work the soup in a blender or
food processor until smooth,
then turn into a bowl, cover and
leave overnight in a cool place or
the refrigerator until cold, to allow
the flavours to develop.

4 To serve (10 minutes): Reheat
the soup until bubbling, then
lower the heat, stir in half the
cream and heat through without
boiling. Taste and adjust the
seasoning.

5 Pour the hot soup into a
warmed tureen or individual
bowls, swirl with the remaining
cream and sprinkle with the grated
orange rind. Serve immediately.

Menu Suggestion
This soup makes an unusual
dinner party starter served with
crisp poppadoms. Follow with
Pork with Cider and Coriander
(page 36) for the main course and
Iced Orange Sabayon (page 79)
for the dessert.

ICED COURGETTE SOUP

| 0.40* | ✳* | 260 cals |

* plus cooling and overnight chilling;
freeze at the end of step 3

Serves 4

50 g (2 oz) butter or margarine

**450 g (1 lb) courgettes, trimmed
and chopped**

1 medium potato, peeled and diced

**750 ml (1¼ pints) vegetable stock or
water**

**5 ml (1 tsp) chopped fresh basil or
2.5 ml (½ tsp) dried basil**

salt and freshly ground pepper

100 g (4 oz) ripe Blue Brie

sliced courgette, to serve (optional)

1 To prepare (35 minutes): Melt
the butter or margarine in a
large heavy-based saucepan. Add
the courgettes and potato, cover
the pan and fry gently for about 10
minutes until softened, shaking
frequently.

2 Add the stock or water with
the basil and seasoning to
taste. Bring to the boil, stirring,
then lower the heat and simmer
for 20 minutes until the vegetables
are tender.

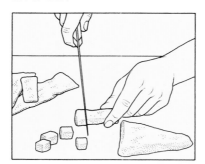

3 Remove the rind from the Brie
and chop the cheese into small
dice. Put into a blender or food
processor, then pour in the soup.
Blend until smooth, then turn into
a bowl, cover and leave until cold.
Chill in the refrigerator overnight.

4 To serve (5 minutes): Whisk
the soup vigorously to ensure
an even consistency, then taste
and adjust seasoning. Pour into a
chilled soup tureen or individual
bowls and float the courgette slices
on the top if liked.

Menu Suggestion
The perfect starter for a summer
dinner party or barbecue. Follow
with Summer Fish Hot Pot (page
48) and finish with Blackberry Ice
Cream (page 78).

Main Meals

The main course of any meal is obviously important. If the main course isn't a success, then most guests will remember the whole meal as a disaster. The cook-ahead dishes in this chapter are designed to help you get it right every time. With the main course organised in advance, there will be no last-minute panics or rush, and meat dishes like casseroles will be greatly improved in flavour.

LAMB AND ORANGE CASSEROLE WITH CHOUX DUMPLINGS

3.25*	❄*	790 cals

* plus cooling overnight; freeze at the end of step 4

Serves 4

45 ml (3 tbsp) vegetable oil

900 g (2 lb) lean boned leg of lamb, trimmed of fat and cubed

1 medium onion, skinned and chopped

2 turnips, peeled and roughly chopped

3 carrots, peeled and roughly chopped

75 g (3 oz) plain flour

15 ml (1 tbsp) tomato purée

300 ml ($\frac{1}{2}$ pint) unsweetened orange juice

150 ml ($\frac{1}{4}$ pint) chicken stock

2 bay leaves

salt and freshly ground pepper

50 g (2 oz) butter

150 ml ($\frac{1}{4}$ pint) water

2 eggs, beaten

finely grated rind of 2 oranges

30 ml (2 tbsp) chopped fresh parsley and orange shreds, to garnish

1 *To prepare* (2 hours): Heat the oil in a large flameproof casserole, add the lamb in batches and fry over brisk heat until browned on all sides. Remove with a slotted spoon and set aside.

2 Add the onion to the casserole, lower the heat and fry gently for 5 minutes until soft but not coloured. Add the turnips and carrots and fry for a further 5 minutes, stirring constantly.

3 Stir 15 g ($\frac{1}{2}$ oz) of the flour into the casserole, then add the tomato purée. Stir for 1–2 minutes, then pour in the orange juice and stock and bring to the boil, stirring.

4 Return the meat to the casserole, add the bay leaves and seasoning to taste and stir well to mix. Cover and cook in the oven at 180°C (350°F) mark 4 for 1$\frac{1}{2}$ hours or until the lamb is just tender. Leave in a cool place overnight.

5 *To serve* (1 hour 25 minutes): Make the choux dumplings. Sift the remaining flour and a a pinch of salt on to a sheet of greaseproof paper. Put the butter in a medium saucepan, add the water and heat gently until the butter has melted.

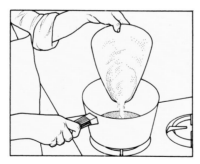

6 Bring the water to a rolling boil and tip in the flour and salt all at once.

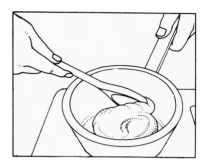

7 Immediately take the pan off the heat and beat vigorously until the mixture forms a ball and leaves the sides of the pan clean.

8 Turn the ball into a bowl and leave to cool for 1–2 minutes, then beat in the eggs a little at a time. The finished paste should be quite stiff.

9 Beat the orange rind and parsley into the choux paste. Remove the bay leaves from the casserole, then pipe or spoon 8 choux balls on top.

10 Bake uncovered in the oven at 200°C (400°F) mark 6 for about 1 hour until the dumplings are risen and golden brown. Serve hot, straight from the casserole, garnished with parsley and orange shreds.

Menu Suggestion
Serve for an informal dinner party with a seasonal green vegetable such as broccoli, Brussels sprouts or green beans.

MARINATED LAMB CUTLETS

1.45* 🍳 £ £ 714 cals

* plus 12 hours marinating and 1 hour cooling

Serves 6

two 1.1 kg (2½ lb) best end necks of lamb, chined

450 ml (¾ pint) dry white wine

200 ml (7 fl oz) vegetable oil

60 ml (4 tbsp) chopped fresh rosemary or 20 ml (4 tsp) dried

5 ml (1 tsp) salt

freshly ground pepper

1 large garlic clove, crushed

700 g (1½ lb) pickling onions, skinned

30 ml (2 tbsp) soft brown sugar

30 ml (2 tbsp) red wine

30 ml (2 tbsp) tomato purée

1 *To prepare* (1 hour 45 minutes): Trim away any excess fat, and remove the flesh between each cutlet bone. Place the meat in a glass or china dish.

2 Mix the white wine, 120 ml (8 tbsp) oil, rosemary, seasoning and crushed garlic together and pour over the meat. Cover and marinate for 12 hours, turning once.

3 While the meat is marinating, heat the remaining vegetable oil in a large frying pan, add the onions with the sugar and stir well. Cook over moderate heat for about 15 minutes until well-browned, shaking the pan occasionally.

4 Add the red wine and tomato purée and bring to the boil. Lower the heat and cook gently, uncovered, for 5–10 minutes until the onions are glazed. Remove from the heat, cool and chill.

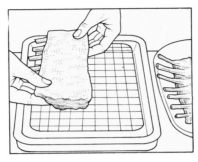

5 Lift the meat out of the marinade and place on a rack standing over a roasting tin.

6 Cook in the oven at 180°C (350°F) mark 4 for about 1½ hours or until the meat is tender, basting occasionally.

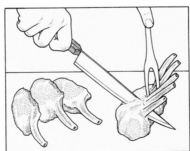

7 While still warm, divide the meat into cutlets and spoon over the marinade. Baste and turn from time to time until cold, about 1 hour. Cover and leave in a cool place until serving time.

8 *To serve*: Arrange the cutlets on a serving plate and garnish with the onions. Serve chilled.

Menu Suggestion
Serve this as a main course for a dinner party. Start with Iced Courgette Soup (page 27); finish with Pommes Bristol (page 73).

BEEF AND CHESTNUT CASSEROLE

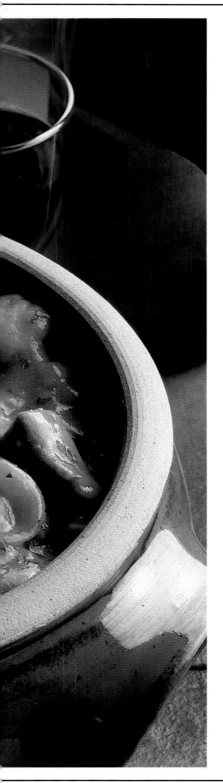

2.45* ✳* 763 cals

* plus overnight cooling; freeze at the end of step 4

Serves 4

45 ml (3 tbsp) vegetable oil

1.1 kg (2½ lb) chuck steak, trimmed of fat and cubed

1 medium onion, skinned and sliced

1 garlic clove, skinned and crushed

30 ml (2 tbsp) plain wholewheat flour

300 ml (½ pint) dry cider

300 ml (½ pint) beef stock

30 ml (2 tbsp) mushroom ketchup

5 ml (1 tsp) dried mixed herbs

salt and freshly ground pepper

439 g (15½ oz) can whole chestnuts in salted water, drained

30 ml (2 tbsp) chopped fresh parsley, to garnish

1 *To prepare* (2 hours 25 minutes): Heat the oil in a large flameproof casserole, add the beef in batches and fry over brisk heat until browned on all sides. Remove with a slotted spoon and set aside.

2 Add the onion and garlic to the casserole, lower the heat and fry gently for 5 minutes until soft but not coloured.

3 Return the meat to the casserole and stir in the flour. Cook, stirring, for 1–2 minutes, then stir in the cider, stock and mushroom ketchup. Bring slowly to the boil, then add the herbs and seasoning to taste.

4 Cover the casserole and cook in the oven at 170°C (325°F) mark 3 for 2 hours or until the beef is tender. Leave in a cool place overnight.

5 *To serve* (20 minutes): Reheat the casserole on top of the cooker until bubbling, then add the chestnuts and heat through for a further 10 minutes. Taste and adjust seasoning and sprinkle with the parsley before serving.

Menu Suggestion
This is a hearty casserole, suitable for a winter dinner party. Start the meal with Smoked Trout Mousse in Lemon Shells (page 14) and finish with Coffee Bavarian Cream (page 77) or Baked Rum and Raisin Cheesecake (page 68).

BEEF AND CHESTNUT CASSEROLE

Cans of whole chestnuts in salted water (brine) are available at most large supermarkets and delicatessens, imported from France. They are very convenient to use and have a good flavour. Their texture is rather soft, however, due to the canning process. If you prefer crunchier chestnuts, then fresh chestnuts can be used, but it is best to cook them beforehand and add them to the casserole just to heat through, otherwise you run the risk of overcooking them. To cook fresh chestnuts: first make a small cut in the rounded part of each shell with the point of a small sharp knife. Put the chestnuts in a saucepan and cover with cold water. Bring to the boil and simmer for 10 minutes, then drain. While the chestnuts are still warm, peel off both the outer shells and the inner skins.

Cook the chestnuts in stock or water to cover for about 20 minutes until tender, then drain before use.

BITKIS

2.00* £ 637 cals

* plus overnight soaking and 2–3 hours cooling

Serves 6

100 g (4 oz) medium oatmeal

300 ml ($\frac{1}{2}$ pint) milk

2 medium onions, roughly chopped

900 g (2 lb) lean minced beef

salt and freshly ground pepper

15 ml (3 tsp) caraway seeds (optional)

75 ml (5 tbsp) seasoned flour

60 ml (4 tbsp) vegetable oil

25 g (1 oz) butter

25 g (1 oz) plain flour

450 ml ($\frac{3}{4}$ pint) beef or chicken stock

30 ml (2 tbsp) tomato purée

300 ml ($\frac{1}{2}$ pint) soured cream

parsley sprigs, to garnish

1 To prepare (40 minutes): Soak the oatmeal in the milk overnight. Squeeze out excess milk and mix the oatmeal with the onions, minced beef and seasoning to taste.

2 Put this mixture twice through a mincer or mix in a food processor until smooth. Beat in 10 ml (2 tsp) of the caraway seeds, if using.

3 Shape into 18 round flat cakes, or bitkis. Coat with seasoned flour.

4 Heat the oil in a large frying pan and brown the bitkis well. Place in a single layer in a large shallow ovenproof dish.

5 Melt the butter in a saucepan, add the flour and cook over low heat, stirring with a wooden spoon, for 2 minutes. Gradually blend in the stock, stirring after each addition to prevent lumps forming. Bring to the boil slowly, then simmer for 2–3 minutes, stirring. Stir in the tomato purée, soured cream and remaining caraway seeds, if using.

6 Pour the sauce over the bitkis and cool for 2–3 hours. Cover with foil and chill in the refrigerator until required.

7 To serve (1 hour 20 minutes): Bake in the oven at 180°C (350°F) mark 4 for about 1$\frac{1}{4}$ hours or until the juices run clear when the bitkis are pierced. Garnish with parsley just before serving.

Menu Suggestion

Serve these Russian beef patties for a family meal with noodles and a mixed salad which includes grated or chopped beetroot.

BEEF KABOBS WITH HORSERADISH RELISH

0.45 £ ✳ 399 cals

Serves 6

700 g (1½ lb) lean minced beef
250 g (9 oz) grated onion
135 ml (9 tbsp) horseradish sauce
45 ml (3 tbsp) chopped fresh thyme
250 g (9 oz) fresh white
  breadcrumbs
salt and freshly ground pepper
1 egg, beaten
plain flour, for coating
150 ml (¼ pint) natural yogurt
120 ml (8 tbsp) finely chopped fresh
  parsley

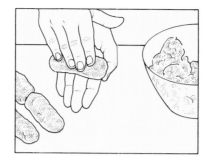

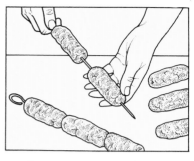

1 To prepare (20 minutes): Place the minced beef in a large bowl and mix in the onion, 90 ml (6 tbsp) of the horseradish, thyme, breadcrumbs and seasoning to taste.

2 Add enough egg to bind the mixture together and, with well-floured hands, shape into 18 even-sized sausages. Cover and chill in the refrigerator until required.

3 To serve (25 minutes): Thread the kabobs lengthways on to 6 oiled skewers. Place under a pre-heated grill and grill for about 20 minutes, turning frequently.

4 Meanwhile, mix the yogurt with the remaining horse-radish and parsley. Serve the kabobs hot, with the sauce handed separately.

Menu Suggestion
Serve Iced Courgette Soup (page 27) for a starter and Mango Mousse for dessert (page 74).

BEEF KABOBS WITH HORSERADISH RELISH

Kabobs—or kebabs as we also call them—are very popular in Indian cookery, and this method of threading minced meat kebabs on skewers is a very common one. In India, such kabobs are cooked on the street, and passers-by stop to buy them and eat them as they are going along. A charcoal grill is used for cooking, which gives them such a wonderful aroma that they are hard to resist if you are hungry when walking by a kabob stall. If you have a barbecue, then cook the kabobs on it, and you will understand why!

PORK WITH CIDER AND CORIANDER

| 0.30 | £ £ | 418 cals |

Serves 4

450 g (1 lb) pork fillet (tenderloin)
1 green pepper
225 g (8 oz) celery
125 g (4 oz) onion, skinned
30 ml (2 tbsp) oil
50 g (2 oz) butter
15 ml (1 tbsp) ground coriander
15 ml (1 tbsp) plain flour
150 ml ($\frac{1}{4}$ pint) dry cider
150 ml ($\frac{1}{4}$ pint) chicken or vegetable stock
salt and freshly ground pepper

1 *To prepare* (15 minutes): Trim and slice the pork fillet into 5 mm ($\frac{1}{4}$ inch) thick pieces. Place between sheets of cling film and bat out thinly. Cover and chill until required.

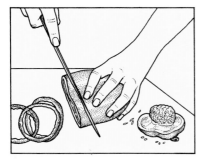

2 Cut the pepper into rings, discarding the core and seeds. Slice the celery into 5 mm ($\frac{1}{4}$ inch) pieces. Chop the onion. Cover the vegetables and chill in the refrigerator until required.

3 *To serve* (15 minutes): Heat the oil with half the butter in a large frying pan. Add the green pepper and celery and fry gently for 2–3 minutes. Lift out with a slotted spoon and keep warm on a serving plate.

4 Add the remaining butter, increase the heat to high, then add the pork, a few pieces at a time. Brown the pork on all sides, then remove from the pan.

5 Add the onion to the residual fat and fry until golden brown. Stir in the coriander and flour and cook for 1 minute. Add the cider and stock and bring quickly to the boil, stirring constantly. Return the pork to the pan, add seasoning to taste and simmer for about 5 minutes. Serve hot, with the green pepper and celery.

Menu Suggestion
This dinner party main course would go well with Stuffed Mushrooms (page 17) to start and Pommes Bristol (page 73) to finish.

PORK WITH CIDER AND CORIANDER
Fillet or tenderloin of pork is a luxury cut of meat, but well worth the expense when you are entertaining, because you can rely on it being beautifully moist and tender, and there are no wasteful bones and fat. The fillet or tenderloin comes from beneath the middle loin and the chump end of the pig—the butcher detaches it and sells it separately rather than including it with middle loin or chump chops. It is an excellent cut for quick pan-frying as in the recipe; it also makes a good roasting joint if two fillets are tied together with a stuffing in between.

ORANGE GLAZED GAMMON

2.35* £ £ 490–613 cals

* plus 2–3 hours soaking and 3–4
  hours cooling

Serves 8–10

1.8 kg (4 lb) corner gammon

30 ml (2 tbsp) Dijon mustard

45 ml (3 tbsp) orange marmalade

1.25 ml ($\frac{1}{4}$ tsp) ground allspice

50 g (2 oz) soft brown sugar

salt and freshly ground pepper

1 orange

whole cloves

pickled walnuts and orange slices,
  to garnish

1 *To prepare* (2 hours
25 minutes): Cover the
gammon with cold water and soak
for 2–3 hours. Drain and calculate
the cooking time, allowing 25
minutes per 450 g (1 lb).

2 Place the joint, skin side down,
in a large pan and cover with
cold water. Bring to the boil, skim
and reduce the heat. Cover
and simmer for half the cooking
time.

3 Drain the joint, wrap in foil,
then place in a roasting tin.
Continue to cook in the oven at
180°C (350°F) mark 4 for the rest
of the calculated time.

4 Make the glaze. Put the
mustard in a bowl with the
marmalade, allspice, sugar and
seasoning to taste. Mix well.

5 Remove the joint from the
oven and increase the oven
temperature to 200°C (400°F)
mark 6.

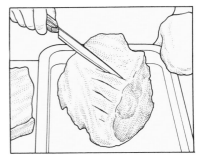

6 Unwrap the joint, strip off the
rind and slash the fat with a
sharp knife. Spread the fat with
half of the glaze. Place the joint in
a foil-lined roasting tin, return to
the oven and cook for 20 minutes.

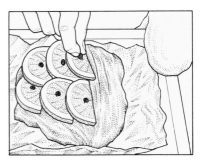

7 Cut the orange into thin slices,
then halve them. Using cloves,
attach the orange pieces to the
joint. Brush with the remaining
glaze. Return to the oven for a
further 10 minutes, then cool for
3–4 hours. Chill in the refrigerator
until required.

8 *To serve* (10 minutes): Carve
into slices and garnish with
pickled walnuts and orange slices.

Menu Suggestion
This cold gammon joint makes a
spectacular centrepiece for a
buffet party table. Serve with
potato salad, apple coleslaw, and
beetroot and orange salad.
Marinated raw mushrooms or
Mushrooms in Red Wine (page
54) would also go well with the
orange-flavoured gammon.

AUBERGINES WITH HAM

1.45 £ 565 cals

Serves 2

2 even-sized aubergines, about
   450 g (1 lb) total weight
vegetable oil
125 g (4 oz) onion, skinned
125 g (4 oz) cooked lean ham
50 g (2 oz) butter
1 garlic clove, skinned and crushed
30 ml (2 tbsp) plain flour
10 ml (2 tsp) chopped fresh basil or
   2.5 ml (½ tsp) dried
50 g (2 oz) fresh white breadcrumbs
5 ml (1 tsp) French mustard
5 ml (1 tsp) lemon juice
60 ml (4 tbsp) single cream
salt and freshly ground pepper

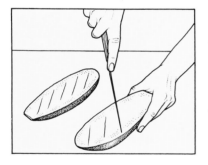

1 To prepare (1 hour 15 minutes):
Cut the aubergines in half
lengthways, then score the
exposed flesh on the cut sides.

2 Brush the aubergines with oil
and place, cut sides upper-
most, in an ovenproof dish. Add
60 ml (4 tbsp) water, cover with
foil or a lid and bake in the oven
at 190°C (375°F) mark 5 for about
50 minutes until the flesh is just
tender. Do not overcook.

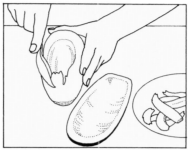

3 With a sharp-edged teaspoon,
scoop out as much flesh from
the aubergines as possible, leaving
the shells intact. Chop the flesh.
Finely chop the onion and ham.

4 Melt half the butter in a saucepan, add the onion and fry
gently until soft. Add the garlic
and aubergine flesh and fry for
2–3 minutes.

5 Sprinkle over the flour and
basil; cook for 2–3 minutes,
stirring. Add the ham, all but
30 ml (2 tbsp) of the breadcrumbs,
the mustard, lemon juice, cream
and seasoning to taste.

6 Fill the aubergine shells with
the stuffing. Top with the
reserved breadcrumbs and dot with
the remaining butter. Cover and
chill in the refrigerator until
required.

7 To serve (30 minutes): Bake in
the oven, uncovered, at 190°C
(375°F) mark 5 for about 30
minutes. Serve hot.

Menu Suggestion
Stuffed aubergines make a light
main course for an informal
supper party. Serve with a mixed
salad, French bread and a bottle of
full-bodied wine, and follow with
a selection of cheeses and grapes,
dates or figs.

SAUSAGE AND EGG PIE

| 1.30 | 🍴 | £ | 626–939 cals |

Serves 4–6

shortcrust pastry (see page 156)
    made with 275 g (10 oz) plain
    flour

3 eggs, hard-boiled

10 ml (2 tsp) horseradish sauce

225 g (8 oz) sausagemeat

2 eggs, beaten

150 ml ($\frac{1}{4}$ pint) single cream or
    milk

5 ml (1 tsp) chopped fresh sage or
    2.5 ml ($\frac{1}{2}$ tsp) dried

salt and freshly ground pepper

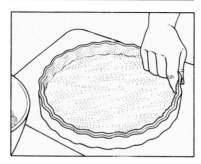

1 *To prepare* (30 minutes): Use two-thirds of the pastry to line a 20.5 cm (8 inch) flan ring placed on a baking sheet.

2 Shell the hard-boiled eggs and halve lengthways. Mix the horseradish sauce with the sausagemeat, divide into 6 and mould over the white of each egg half. Place yolk side down in the flan case.

3 Reserve 10 ml (2 tsp) of the beaten eggs for glazing, then mix the remainder with the cream, sage and seasoning to taste. Pour into the flan case.

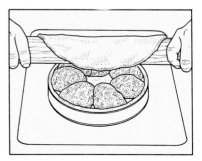

4 Cover with the remaining pastry, sealing the edges well. Decorate with pastry trimmings. Chill in the refrigerator until required.

5 *To serve* (1 hour): Glaze the pie with the reserved beaten eggs, then bake in the oven at 170°C (325°F) mark 3 for about 1 hour. Serve hot or cold.

Menu Suggestion

Sausage and Egg Pie makes a filling dish for a family supper. Serve hot with French beans tossed in melted herb butter, or baked beans if there are children eating. For a picnic or summer meal in the garden, serve the pie cold with a selection of salads.

SAUSAGE AND EGG PIE

This pie makes a filling family meal from everyday ingredients, yet shows you have gone to a little more trouble than simply giving them sausage and eggs! For best results, choose a good-quality sausagemeat which is not too fatty. Some varieties, especially those that the butcher make himself, have herbs and spices added, which would give the filling a tasty flavour. Served cold, this pie is also excellent for picnics and packed lunches.

CHICKEN POT PIES

| 3.00* | ✳* | 847 cals |

* plus cooling overnight; freeze without pastry glaze in step 10

Serves 4

1.1 kg (2½ lb) chicken, giblets removed

1 lemon

few sprigs of fresh tarragon or 2.5 ml (½ tsp) dried

1 bay leaf

salt and freshly ground pepper

2 leeks, trimmed and sliced

2 large carrots, peeled and thinly sliced

175 g (6 oz) button onions, topped and tailed

40 g (1½ oz) butter or margarine

175 g (6 oz) button mushrooms, wiped and halved or sliced if large

45 ml (3 tbsp) plain flour

60 ml (4 tbsp) double cream

368 g (13 oz) packet frozen puff pastry, thawed

a little beaten egg, to glaze

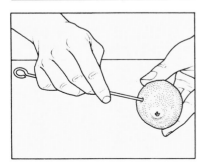

1 To prepare (2 hours 15 minutes): Wash the chicken inside and out. Prick the lemon all over with a skewer, then place inside the chicken.

2 Put the chicken in a large saucepan with the tarragon, bay leaf and seasoning to taste. Add the giblets (except the liver), then pour in just enough water to cover the chicken and bring slowly to the boil. Lower the heat, half cover with a lid and simmer for 1¼ hours or until tender.

3 Add the leeks and carrots for the last 30 minutes of the cooking time. Remove the pan from the heat and leave the chicken and vegetables to cool in the liquid.

4 Remove the chicken from the cooking liquid. Cut the flesh from the bird, discarding all skin and bones. Dice the flesh into bite-sized pieces. Set aside.

5 Place the button onions in a bowl, pour in boiling water to cover and leave for 2–3 minutes. Drain and plunge into cold water, then remove the onions one at a time and peel off the skins with your fingers.

6 Melt the butter or margarine in a clean saucepan, add the onions and fry gently for 5 minutes until lightly coloured.

7 Strain the cooking liquid from the chicken, measure and reserve 300 ml (½ pint). Add the mushrooms to the onions, together with the leeks and carrots, discarding the tarragon sprigs, if used, and the bay leaf. Fry the vegetables gently for 1–2 minutes, then add the chicken pieces and fry for a few minutes more.

8 Mix the flour to a paste with the cream. Gradually blend in the measured cooking liquid, then pour into the pan of chicken and vegetables. Add seasoning to taste. Simmer, stirring, for 2–3 minutes, then turn into four 300 ml (½ pint) ovenproof pie dishes. Cover and leave until completely cold, overnight if convenient.

9 To serve (45 minutes): Roll out the pastry on a floured surface and cut out four circles or ovals to make lids. Cut four strips of pastry long enough to go around the rims of the dishes.

10 Dampen the rims of the pie dishes then place the strips of pastry around them. Dampen the pastry strips, then place the circles of pastry on top. Press firmly to seal, then knock up and flute. Make a hole in the centre of each pie and decorate with pastry trimmings if liked. Glaze with beaten egg.

11 Bake the pies in the oven at 200°C (400°F) mark 6 for 25 minutes or until the pastry is golden brown and the filling heated through. Serve hot.

Menu Suggestion
These individual pies are perfect for an informal supper party, served simply with a tossed mixed salad and beer, lager or wine. Follow with a selection of different cheeses and fresh fruit.

CHICKEN AND REDCURRANT CURRY

| 1.30* | ✳ | 441 cals |

* plus 2–3 hours cooling

Serves 4

4 chicken leg joints

350 g (12 oz) onions, skinned and roughly chopped

2.5 cm (1 inch) piece fresh root ginger, peeled and finely chopped

2 garlic cloves, skinned and crushed

30 ml (2 tbsp) vegetable oil

10 ml (2 tsp) ground cumin

10 ml (2 tsp) ground coriander

5 ml (1 tsp) chilli powder

2.5 ml ($\frac{1}{2}$ tsp) ground turmeric

30 ml (2 tbsp) lemon juice

100 g (4 oz) redcurrant jelly

200 ml ($\frac{1}{3}$ pint) chicken stock

salt and freshly ground pepper

2 bay leaves

coriander sprigs, to garnish

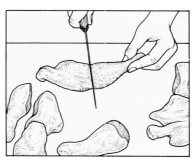

1 *To prepare* (1 hour 10 minutes): Cut the chicken legs into thighs and drumsticks; remove skin and fat.

2 In a blender or food processor, work the onions, ginger and garlic together until fairly smooth.

3 Heat the oil in large heavy-based pan, add the onion paste and fry gently until golden. Add the chicken joints and fry until golden on all sides.

4 Add the cumin, coriander, chilli, turmeric and lemon juice. Cook for 5 minutes until the chicken pieces are evenly coated with spices, then stir in the redcurrant jelly, stock and seasoning to taste. Bring to the boil, add the bay leaves, cover and simmer for 45–50 minutes or until the chicken is tender.

5 Remove from the heat, leave to cool for 2–3 hours, then cover and chill in the refrigerator until required.

6 *To serve* (20 minutes): Bring to the boil on top of the cooker, then lower the heat and simmer gently for 10–15 minutes to heat through. Taste and adjust seasoning and garnish with coriander just before serving.

Menu Suggestion

Serve as part of an Indian-style meal with Curried Parsnip and Orange Soup (page 26) to start and Mango Mousse (page 74) to follow. The curry itself is best served with plain boiled rice and side dishes of sliced banana and coconut, yogurt and cucumber, mango chutney and lime pickle.

CHICKEN AND REDCURRANT CURRY

If you have time, the chicken in this recipe would benefit from being marinated in the onion, ginger and garlic paste. After skinning the chicken, make a few slashes in the flesh with the tip of a sharp knife, then place in a bowl and spread with the paste. If you like, you can add the juice of 1 lime or $\frac{1}{2}$ a lemon. Leave for at least 1 hour, or overnight in the refrigerator if possible. Fry the paste and chicken together in step 3, then continue as in the recipe above.

CHICKEN AND CAPER CROQUETTES

1.00* 🍳 £ 302 cals

* plus 30 minutes cooling and several hours chilling

Makes 12

1.4 kg (3 lb) chicken, poached
100 g (4 oz) butter
100 g (4 oz) plain flour
568 ml (1 pint) milk
30 ml (2 tbsp) chopped fresh tarragon or 10 ml (2 tsp) dried
15 ml (1 tbsp) chopped fresh parsley
30 ml (2 tbsp) chopped capers
salt and freshly ground pepper
2 eggs, beaten
50 g (2 oz) fresh white breadcrumbs
25 g (1 oz) chopped almonds
vegetable oil, for frying

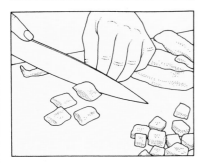

1 To prepare (45 minutes): Remove the flesh from the cold chicken and dice roughly.

2 Melt the butter in a saucepan, add the flour and cook over low heat, stirring with a wooden spoon, for 2 minutes. Gradually blend in the milk, stirring after each addition to prevent lumps forming. Bring to the boil slowly, then simmer for at least 10 minutes, until very thick. Stir in the tarragon, parsley and capers. Season well and leave to cool for 30 minutes.

3 Stir in the chicken and spread the mixture out on a large flat plate. Chill in the refrigerator for several hours.

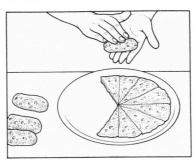

4 Divide the mixture into 12 equal sections. Shape each into a croquette 6.5 cm (2½ inch) long, using floured hands.

5 Brush each croquette evenly with beaten egg. Mix the breadcrumbs and almonds together and use to coat the croquettes. Pat well in, to coat thoroughly and evenly. Chill in the refrigerator until required.

6 To serve (15 minutes): Deep fry in oil at 180°C (350°F) for 4–5 minutes or shallow fry for about 6–7 minutes until golden brown. Drain well on absorbent kitchen paper before serving.

Menu Suggestion

These croquettes make a tasty everyday main course for the family. Serve with a mixed salad tossed in lots of blue cheese dressing, or with coleslaw. Children will probably enjoy them best with French fries.

CASSEROLED TURKEY IN RED WINE

| 3.20* | ✳ | 434–495 cals |

* plus 2–3 hours cooling

Serves 4

25 g (1 oz) butter

30 ml (2 tbsp) vegetable oil

450–700 g (1–1½ lb) turkey casserole meat

125 g (4 oz) lean streaky bacon, rinded and diced

30 ml (2 tbsp) plain flour

good pinch of dried thyme

1 bay leaf

150 ml (¼ pint) red wine

300 ml (½ pint) water (or unseasoned stock)

salt and freshly ground pepper

12 small onions or shallots, skinned

chopped fresh parsley and pastry crescents or croûtons, to serve

1 *To prepare* (2 hours 30 minutes): Melt half the butter with half the oil in a large frying pan. When foaming, add the turkey meat and brown well. Remove with a slotted spoon and place in a casserole.

2 Add the bacon to the frying pan and fry until beginning to brown. Remove the bacon with a slotted spoon and add to the turkey.

3 Stir the flour, thyme and bay leaf into the fat left in the frying pan and cook gently for a few minutes. Slowly stir in the red wine, water and seasoning to taste. Bring to the boil, stirring, then pour over the turkey.

4 Cover the casserole tightly and cook in the oven at 150°C (300°F) mark 2, for about 2 hours.

5 Thirty minutes before the end of the cooking time, melt the remaining butter and oil in a frying pan. Add the onions and cook slowly until golden brown and tender. Add the onions to the casserole, cool for 2–3 hours, then chill in the refrigerator until required.

6 *To serve* (20–50 minutes): Place the casserole on top of the cooker, slowly bring to the boil, then lower the heat and simmer for 20 minutes.

7 Alternatively, reheat in the oven at 220°C (425°F) mark 7 for 30 minutes or until boiling, then at 150°C (300°F) mark 2 for 20 minutes. Garnish with parsley and pastry crescents or croûtons and serve hot.

Menu Suggestion

Serve for a dinner party with Stuffed Mushrooms (page 17) to start and Sherried Apricot Trifle (page 70) to finish.

CASSEROLED TURKEY IN RED WINE

Small pickling onions and shallots are not always easy to obtain all year round, yet they do look attractive whole in this casserole. If you are unable to get them, use 2 medium onions, skinned and chopped, and fry them with the diced bacon in step 2 of the recipe. To improve the appearance of the finished dish, add 100–175 g (4–6 oz) whole button mushrooms in step 5 instead of the whole onions.

SUMMER FISH HOT POT

1.10*	£	459 cals

* plus 30 minutes cooling

Serves 4

4 sticks of celery, washed and
    trimmed

50 g (2 oz) butter

50 g (2 oz) plain flour

450 ml ($\frac{3}{4}$ pint) milk

salt and freshly ground pepper

700 g (1$\frac{1}{2}$ lb) firm white fish fillets
    (cod, haddock or monkfish)

275 g (10 oz) Florence fennel,
    untrimmed weight

60 ml (4 tbsp) chopped parsley

10 ml (2 tsp) lemon juice

450 g (1 lb) new potatoes, boiled

chopped fresh parsley, to garnish

1 *To prepare* (20 minutes): Slice
the celery finely. Melt
the butter in a flameproof
casserole, add the celery and cook
gently for 5 minutes until soft.
Add the flour and cook over low
heat, stirring with a wooden
spoon, for 2 minutes. Remove
from the heat and gradually blend
in the milk, stirring after each
addition to prevent lumps
forming. Bring to the boil slowly,
then simmer for 2–3 minutes,
stirring. Add seasoning to taste
and remove from the heat.

2 Place the fish in a saucepan
and just cover with water.
Bring to the boil, remove from the
heat and drain. Cut into fork-size
pieces, discarding the skin and any
bones.

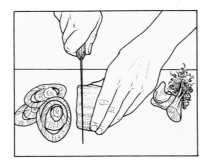

3 Trim the fennel and cut into
thin slices. Blanch in boiling
salted water for 2 minutes and
drain.

4 Add the fennel, parsley and
lemon juice to the sauce; mix
well. Stir in the fish, taking care
not to break up the flesh; cool for
30 minutes.

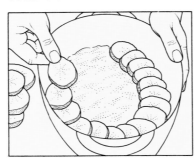

5 Slice the cooked potatoes and
arrange on top of the fish.
Cover the dish with buttered foil
and chill in the refrigerator until
required.

6 *To serve* (50 minutes): Bake in
the oven, with foil covering, at
180°C (350°F) mark 4 for about 50
minutes or until the fish is cooked.
Sprinkle with chopped parsley
before serving.

Menu Suggestion
This Mediterranean style fish stew
contains fennel and potatoes, and
so does not need a vegetable
accompaniment. Serve for an
informal meal with crusty fresh
bread or bread rolls, and a
bottle of chilled dry white wine.

CREAMED SEAFOOD VOL-AU-VENTS

0.55*	✳*	684 cals

* plus cooling and overnight chilling of filling; freeze filling at the end of step 5

Serves 4

450 g (1 lb) monkfish or haddock
　fillets
1 bay leaf
few black peppercorns
few parsley sprigs
1 slice of onion
300 ml ($\frac{1}{2}$ pint) milk
25 g (1 oz) butter or margarine
25 g (1 oz) flour
150 ml ($\frac{1}{4}$ pint) single cream
100 g (4 oz) Gruyère cheese, finely
　grated
1.25 ml ($\frac{1}{4}$ tsp) ground mace or
　grated nutmeg
salt and freshly ground pepper
225 g (8 oz) prawns, defrosted and
　thoroughly dried if frozen
16 medium-sized (6.5 cm/2$\frac{1}{2}$ inch)
　frozen vol-au-vent cases
beaten egg, to glaze

1 *To prepare* (30 minutes): Put the monkfish or haddock in a saucepan with the bay leaf, peppercorns, parsley and onion. Pour over the milk, then bring to the boil. Cover tightly, remove from the heat and leave until cold.

2 Remove the fish from the cooking liquid and reserve. Flake the flesh of the fish roughly, discarding the skin and any bones. Set aside.

3 Melt the butter or margarine in a heavy-based saucepan. Sprinkle in the flour and cook, stirring, for 1–2 minutes.

4 Remove from the heat and stir in the strained cooking liquid a little at a time, whisking vigorously until smooth. Simmer gently for 2 minutes, then add the cream and 75 g (3 oz) of the Gruyère cheese. Stir over very low heat until the cheese has melted.

5 Turn the sauce into a bowl and add the mace or nutmeg and seasoning to taste. Gently fold in the flaked white fish and the prawns. Cover the surface of the sauce closely with cling film, leave until cold, then chill overnight.

6 *To serve* (25 minutes): Place the frozen vol-au-vent cases on a dampened baking sheet and brush the rims carefully with beaten egg. Bake in the oven at 220°C (425°F) mark 7 for about 15 minutes or according to packet instructions.

7 Meanwhile reheat the filling gently in a heavy-based saucepan until hot and bubbling. Taste and adjust seasoning.

8 Remove the soft centres from the vol-au-vent cases, spoon in the filling, then replace the crisp tops. Serve piping hot.

Menu Suggestion
These vol-au-vents are rather special. Serve them as an impressive dinner party main course with a green vegetable such as mange-touts, or courgettes tossed in melted butter and the finely grated rind and juice of a lime. Start the meal with Terrine of Chicken with Wine (page 9) and finish with Iced Orange Sabayon (page 79).

CREAMED SEAFOOD VOL-AU-VENTS

Frozen uncooked vol-au-vent cases, available at supermarkets and freezer centres, are an absolute boon to the busy cook, because you can quite literally take them from the packet and pop them in the oven—and you get perfectly shaped and beautifully risen vol-au-vents every time. Different manu-facturers sell different sizes, so you must check carefully before buying. Cocktail vol-au-vents are usually about a bite-sized 5 cm (2 inches) in diameter, medium size are 6.5 cm (2$\frac{1}{2}$ inches), large are 9 cm (3$\frac{1}{2}$ inches), and king size are 9.5 cm (3$\frac{3}{4}$ inches). The medium size are the ones most widely available, and the ones to use for most main course dishes—allow four per serving. Large and king size vol-au-vents, while a good size for individual servings, are sometimes difficult to obtain.

Vegetables and Salads

Most vegetable and salad dishes need to be prepared just before serving to retain maximum crispness and freshness, but this doesn't mean that you have to leave everything to the last minute. Plan to do at least one vegetable or salad dish in advance—this is especially important when entertaining, as it will give you more time to enjoy the company of your guests.

GRUYÈRE POTATOES

2.35* £ ✳ 303 cals

Serves 6

900 g (2 lb) potatoes
25 g (1 oz) butter
125 g (4 oz) Gruyère cheese, grated
freshly grated nutmeg
salt and freshly ground pepper
568 ml (1 pint) milk

1 *To prepare* (1 hour 50 minutes): Peel the potatoes, then slice thinly. (Do not soak them in cold water.)

2 Use a little of the butter to lightly grease a 1.4 litre (2½ pint) shallow ovenproof dish.

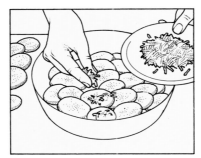

3 Layer the potatoes and most of the cheese in the dish. Add a generous grating of nutmeg, and seasoning to taste.

4 Top with cheese and then pour over the milk, which should just cover the potatoes.

5 Dot the surface with the remaining butter. Cover with foil and bake in the oven at 180°C (350°F) mark 4 for about 1½ hours or until the potatoes are quite tender and most of the milk has been absorbed. Cool, cover with clean foil and chill in the refrigerator until required.

6 *To serve* (45 minutes): Uncover and bake in the oven at 180°C (350°F) mark 4 for 45 minutes until the top is golden brown. Serve hot.

Menu Suggestion
Gruyère potatoes are a special occasion dish. Serve them for a dinner party with a main course of roast meat or a casserole, which can be cooked in the oven at the same time.

GRUYÈRE POTATOES

Gruyère potatoes are a variation of the famous French potato dish called *gratin dauphinois*, in which the potatoes are cooked in cream, rather than milk as suggested here. For a special occasion, you can use cream, or a combination of cream and milk, which will be less rich — and less expensive. Some French cooks add finely chopped onion and crushed garlic to this dish, which give it a good flavour.

Cheddar cheese can be used for an everyday occasion, but it does not give such a good melt-in-the-mouth texture as Gruyère. When preparing the potatoes for baked dishes such as this one, it is very important to slice them as thinly as possible. For a simpler, less rich dish, try Layered French-Style Potatoes (page 138), which has a mustardy flavour.

MUSHROOMS IN RED WINE

1.05*	131 cals

* plus about 4 hours marinating and overnight chilling

Serves 4

350 g (12 oz) small button mushrooms

300 ml ($\frac{1}{2}$ pint) red wine

15 ml (1 tbsp) crushed coriander seeds

salt and freshly ground pepper

30 ml (2 tbsp) olive oil

1 small onion, skinned and finely chopped

1 garlic clove, skinned and crushed

15 ml (1 tbsp) tomato purée

30 ml (2 tbsp) chopped fresh coriander or continental parsley

8 lettuce leaves, to serve

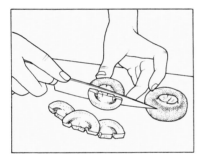

1 *To prepare* (30 minutes): Wipe the mushrooms with a damp cloth; leave them whole if they are very small, otherwise halve them or cut them into even slices.

2 Put the mushrooms in a bowl with the red wine, coriander seeds and seasoning to taste. Cover and leave to marinate for about 4 hours.

3 Heat the olive oil in a heavy-based frying pan. Add the onion and fry gently for 5 minutes until soft but not coloured. Add the garlic and tomato purée and fry for 2 minutes more.

4 Drain the marinade from the mushrooms and reserve. Add the mushrooms to the frying pan, increase the heat and fry, stirring, for 2 minutes until the juices run.

5 Pour the reserved marinade into the pan and bring to boiling point. Remove from the heat, turn into a bowl and leave until cold. Cover with cling film and chill in the refrigerator overnight.

6 *To serve* (35 minutes): Stir the coriander or parsley into the mushrooms. Leave to stand at room temperature for about 30 minutes, then taste and adjust seasoning. Place 2 lettuce leaves in each of 4 individual dishes and spoon the mushrooms on them. Serve immediately or the lettuce will become limp.

Menu Suggestion

With their pungent sauce, these mushrooms make a tasty side dish to serve with cold meats, especially pork and ham. They are also good served as a starter, with crusty French bread and butter.

MUSHROOMS IN RED WINE

Do you know how good mushrooms are for you? They contain more protein per 100 g (4 oz) than most other vegetables, and are also rich in vitamins B1, B2 and B6, and in the minerals potassium, copper and phosphorus. With no cholesterol and no carbohydrate, and only 7 calories per 100 g (4 oz), they're also good for slimmers, especially when eaten raw. To obtain the full food value from cultivated mushrooms, don't wash or peel them; wipe with a damp cloth.

WATERCRESS AND OATMEAL CROQUETTES

| 1.05* | □ | £ | ✳ | 425 cals |

* plus at least 30 minutes chilling

Serves 4

700 g (1½ lb) floury potatoes

15 g (½ oz) butter, softened

1 bunch watercress

2 eggs

salt and freshly ground pepper

15 ml (1 tbsp) plain flour

50 g (2 oz) fresh breadcrumbs

50 g (2 oz) medium oatmeal

vegetable oil, for deep frying

1 *To prepare* (50 minutes): Scrub the potatoes and boil in their skins until tender; about 20 minutes. Drain well.

2 Peel the potatoes, then sieve them into a bowl or mash *well*. Beat in the butter.

3 Wash, drain and finely chop the watercress. Add to the bowl with 1 egg and seasoning to taste; mix well.

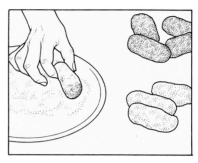

4 Mould the potato mixture into 12 cork-shaped pieces. Coat each croquette lightly in flour.

5 Break the remaining egg on to a plate; beat lightly. Combine the breadcrumbs and oatmeal on another plate.

6 Brush the croquettes with the beaten egg, then coat in the breadcrumb mixture, pressing it on firmly. Chill in the refrigerator for at least 30 minutes or until required.

7 *To serve* (15 minutes): Heat the oil in a deep fat frier to 190°C (375°F). Deep fry the croquettes for about 4 minutes or until golden brown on all sides. Drain on absorbent kitchen paper before serving.

Menu Suggestion

These croquettes make an unusual, colourful alternative to potatoes, and go especially well with lamb and fish dishes.

SALSIFY AU GRATIN

0.45* £ ✳ 316 cals

* plus 30 minutes cooling

Serves 4

450 g (1 lb) salsify, trimmed and peeled

300 ml (½ pint) chicken stock

25 g (1 oz) butter

45 ml (3 tbsp) plain flour

2.5 ml (½ tsp) mustard powder

175 g (6 oz) mature Cheddar cheese, grated

salt and freshly ground pepper

50 g (2 oz) fresh breadcrumbs

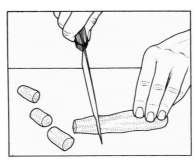

1 To prepare (20 minutes): Cut the salsify into 2.5 cm (1 inch) lengths and place in a saucepan with the stock.

2 Bring to the boil, cover and simmer gently for 15–20 minutes until tender. Drain, reserving the stock, and place the salsify in an overproof dish.

3 Melt the butter in a saucepan, add the flour and mustard powder and cook over low heat, stirring with a wooden spoon, for 2 minutes. Remove the pan from the heat and gradually blend in the reserved stock, stirring after each addition to prevent lumps forming.

4 Bring to the boil slowly, then simmer for 2–3 minutes, stirring. Add half the cheese and seasoning to taste and pour over the salsify.

5 Mix the remaining cheese with the breadcrumbs and sprinkle over the dish. Cool for 30 minutes, cover and chill in the refrigerator until required.

6 To serve (25 minutes): Uncover and bake in the oven at 190°C (375°F) mark 5 for 20–25 minutes until the top is golden brown. Serve hot.

Menu Suggestion

Hot, cheesy and bubbling, this unusual vegetable dish taste delicious with plain roast meats, and can be cooked in the oven at the same time. Try it with the Sunday roast for a change.

SALSIFY AU GRATIN

Salsify is an inexpensive winter vegetable. It looks rather like a long, thin parsnip, and has a soft, white flesh. Years ago it used to be nicknamed the 'vegetable oyster', because its flavour was thought to be similar to that of oysters. Try coating chunks of salsify in batter after parboiling, then deep-frying them as a tasty alternative to chips.

CHILLI POTATO SALAD

| 0.35* | £ | 448 cals |

* plus 2 hours chilling

Serves 6

900 g (2 lb) even-sized new potatoes

1 medium green pepper

1 medium red pepper

200 ml (7 fl oz) vegetable oil

75 ml (5 tbsp) garlic vinegar

15 ml (1 tbsp) chilli seasoning

salt and freshly ground pepper

1 medium onion, skinned and chopped

30 ml (2 tbsp) sesame seeds

fresh coriander, to garnish

1 *To prepare* (30 minutes): Scrub the potatoes and boil in their skins until tender; about 20 minutes. Drain well.

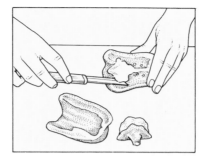

2 Meanwhile, halve, seed and chop the peppers. Blanch them in boiling water for 1–2 minutes. Drain well.

3 In a large bowl, whisk together the oil, vinegar, chilli seasoning and salt and pepper to taste.

4 Halve the potatoes if they are large, but do not peel them. While still hot, stir into the dressing with the onion and peppers. Cool, cover and chill in the refrigerator for about 2 hours.

5 *To serve* (5 minutes): Toast the sesame seeds under the grill, leave to cool, then stir through the salad. Taste and adjust the seasoning before serving, garnished with fresh coriander.

Menu Suggestion
Serve this spicy potato salad with cold meats for lunch, or as a vegetable accompaniment to barbecued chicken or steak.

CAULIFLOWER, BEAN AND CAPER SALAD

2.40* £ 353 cals

* plus overnight soaking and 4 hours standing

Serves 4

175 g (6 oz) dried red kidney beans, soaked in cold water overnight

1 small onion, skinned and finely chopped

1–2 garlic cloves, skinned and crushed

45 ml (3 tbsp) olive oil

15 ml (1 tbsp) red wine vinegar

5 ml (1 tsp) French mustard

salt and freshly ground pepper

225 g (8 oz) cauliflower

60 ml (4 tbsp) natural yogurt or soured cream

60 ml (4 tbsp) mayonnaise

30 ml (2 tbsp) roughly chopped capers

30 ml (2 tbsp) chopped fresh parsley

1 To prepare (2 hours): Drain and rinse the kidney beans, then place in a pan with plenty of water. Bring to the boil and boil rapidly for 10 minutes (this is important—see box). Lower the heat, half cover with a lid and simmer for 1½ hours or until the beans are tender.

2 Drain the beans, transfer to a bowl and immediately add the onion, garlic, olive oil, wine vinegar, mustard and seasoning to taste. Stir well to mix, then cover and leave for at least 4 hours to allow the dressing to flavour the beans.

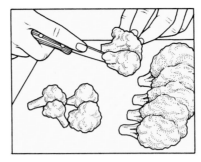

3 To serve (40 minutes): Divide the cauliflower into small sprigs, cutting away all tough stalks. Wash the florets thoroughly under cold running water, then blanch in boiling water for 1 minute only. Drain thoroughly.

4 Add the cauliflower florets to the bean salad with the yogurt or soured cream, mayonnaise, capers and parsley. Mix well and chill in the refrigerator for 30 minutes before serving.

Menu Suggestion

This colourful salad makes a delicious lunch dish served with crusty wholemeal or granary bread, and the combination of pulse and grain provides first-class protein, thus making it a most nutritious meal.

CAULIFLOWER, BEAN AND CAPER SALAD

Dried red kidneys beans *must* be boiled fast for the first 10 minutes of their cooking time. This is to make sure of destroying a poisonous enzyme they contain, which can cause stomach upsets. This fast boiling only applies to red kidney beans, other dried pulses can be boiled in the normal way. If you are short of time for making this salad, you can of course use canned red kidney beans, but they will not absorb the flavour of the dressing so well.

ORIENTAL RICE RING

| 1.00* | 565 cals |

* plus at least 4 hours or overnight chilling

Serves 4

225 g (8 oz) brown rice

salt and freshly ground pepper

40 g (1½ oz) creamed coconut

105 ml (7 tbsp) vegetable oil

15 ml (1 tbsp) soy sauce

15 ml (1 tbsp) wine vinegar

5 ml (1 tsp) clear honey

2 carrots

1 red pepper

75 g (3 oz) beansprouts

25 g (1 oz) unsalted peanuts, chopped

15 ml (1 tbsp) lemon juice

1 To prepare (40 minutes): Cook the brown rice in plenty of boiling salted water until tender: about 30 minutes or according to packet instructions.

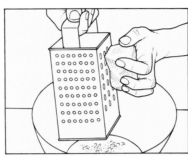

2 Meanwhile, grate the creamed coconut into a bowl. Add 60 ml (4 tbsp) of the oil, the soy sauce, vinegar and honey and beat well to mix.

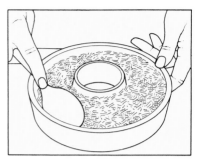

3 Drain the rice well and tip into the bowl of dressing. Stir quickly to mix, add seasoning to taste, then spoon into a lightly oiled 900 ml (1½ pint) ring mould. Press down well, cover and chill in the refrigerator for at least 4 hours, or overnight if more convenient.

4 To serve (20 minutes): Prepare the vegetables. Scrape the carrots, then grate them finely. Cut the red pepper in half, remove the core and seeds, then cut the flesh into thin strips.

5 Combine the carrots, red pepper, beansprouts and peanuts with the remaining oil and the lemon juice. Add seasoning to taste.

6 Turn the rice ring out on to a flat serving plate. Pile the salad in the centre just before serving.

Menu Suggestion

This attractive salad makes a most nutritious lunch served with granary bread rolls, cheese and a green salad.

CUCUMBER SALAD

| 1.10* | 128 cals |

* plus 4 hours or overnight chilling

Serves 4

1 large cucumber
salt and freshly ground pepper
45 ml (3 tbsp) white wine vinegar
45 ml (3 tbsp) water
25 g (1 oz) sugar
2.5 ml ($\frac{1}{2}$ tsp) dried dillweed
150 ml ($\frac{1}{4}$ pint) soured cream
150 ml ($\frac{1}{4}$ pint) thick set natural
  yogurt
30 ml (2 tbsp) snipped chives

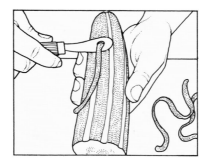

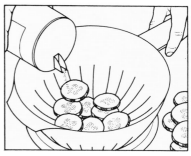

1 To prepare (1 hour): Using a cannelle knife or vegetable peeler, peel lengthways strips off the cucumber. Slice the cucumber thinly into rings.

2 Put the cucumber slices in a colander, sprinkling each layer liberally with salt. Cover with a plate, place heavy weights on top, then leave for 30 minutes.

3 Meanwhile make the dressing. Put the vinegar, water and sugar in a saucepan and heat gently. Boil for 1 minute, remove from the heat and leave to cool.

4 Rinse the cucumber slices quickly under cold running water, then pat dry; place in a bowl. Stir the dill into the dressing with plenty of pepper, then pour over the cucumber. Cover and chill for 4 hours or overnight, turning the slices occasionally.

5 To serve (10 minutes): Mix the soured cream and yogurt with the chives; season to taste. Arrange the cucumber on a serving plate; spoon the dressing in the centre. Serve chilled.

Menu Suggestion
Cucumber Salad is popular in Scandinavian countries, where it is usually served with fish.

LEMONY BEAN SALAD

2.00*	312 cals

* plus overnight soaking and 4 hours standing

Serves 4

100 g (4 oz) green flageolet beans (see box), soaked in cold water overnight

90 ml (6 tbsp) olive oil

finely grated rind and juice of 1 lemon

1–2 garlic cloves, skinned and crushed

salt and freshly ground pepper

50 g (2 oz) black olives

30 ml (2 tbsp) chopped mixed fresh herbs, e.g. basil, marjoram, lemon balm, chives

4 large firm tomatoes

about 1.25 ml ($\frac{1}{4}$ tsp) sugar

1 To prepare (1 hour 30 minutes): Drain and rinse the beans, then place in a pan with plenty of water. Bring to the boil, then lower the heat, half cover with a lid and simmer for about 1 hour until tender.

2 Drain the beans, transfer to a bowl and immediately add the oil, lemon rind and juice, garlic and seasoning to taste. Stir well to mix, then cover and leave for at least 4 hours to allow the dressing to flavour the beans.

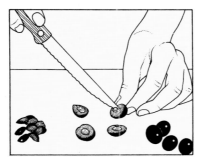

3 To serve (30 minutes): Stone the olives, then chop roughly. Add to the salad with the herbs, then taste and adjust seasoning.

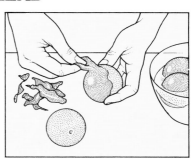

4 Skin the tomatoes. Put them in a bowl, pour over boiling water and leave for 2 minutes. Drain, then plunge into a bowl of cold water. Remove the tomatoes one at a time and peel off the skin with your fingers.

5 Slice the tomatoes thinly, then arrange on 4 serving plates. Sprinkle with sugar and seasoning to taste. Pile the bean salad on top of each plate. Serve chilled.

Menu Suggestion
Fresh and tangy, this summer salad can be served on its own as a starter or light lunch dish, or as an accompaniment to cold meats, especially cold roast chicken or turkey.

LEMONY BEAN SALAD
Green flageolet beans are a very pretty, delicate light green in colour. They are haricot beans which have been removed from their pods when very young and tender, and they get their name from the French word for flute, which they are said to resemble in shape. Most large supermarkets stock green flageolets, but health food shops probably have the fastest turnover. It is important that they have not been stored for too long because, like all dried pulses, they become stale and will not soften, no matter how long you cook them.

Desserts

The last course of any meal is the first one to think of when preparing in advance. Apart from the fact that most desserts are delicious served cold, you should also remember that by the time you've finished eating the main course, you simply won't feel like leaving the table to start cooking all over again. How much more sensible to have the dessert ready to carry to the table—and collect all the compliments.

RASPBERRY ALMOND FLAN

| 1.50* | 🍴 | ✳ | 568 cals |

* plus 1 hour cooling

Serves 8

225 g (8 oz) plain flour

225 g (8 oz) butter or margarine

125 g (4 oz) light soft brown sugar

2 eggs, separated

125 g (4 oz) self-raising flour

75 g (3 oz) ground almonds

60 ml (4 tbsp) milk

225 g (8 oz) raspberries

**150 ml (¼ pint) whipping cream,
    to serve**

1 *To prepare* (1 hour 35 minutes):
Sift the plain flour into a bowl.
Rub in half the fat until the
mixture resembles fine breadcrumbs. Bind to a firm dough
with 60 ml (4 tbsp) water.

2 Knead the dough lightly on a
floured surface, then roll out
and use to line a 25 cm (10 inch)
loose-based fluted flan tin.

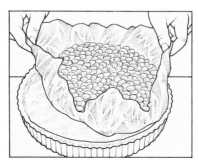

3 Bake blind in the oven at
200°C (400°F) mark 6 for 15–
20 minutes until set but not
browned.

4 Meanwhile beat the remaining
fat with the sugar until light
and fluffy. Gradually beat in the
egg yolks. Gently stir in the self-
raising flour, ground almonds and
milk. Whisk the egg whites until
stiff, then fold into the mixture.

5 Spoon the cake mixture into
the baked flan case and level
the surface. Spinkle over the
raspberries, reserving a few for
decoration.

6 Bake in the oven at 180°C
(350°F) mark 4 for 40–45
minutes or until the flan is golden
brown and firm to the touch. Cool
completely—about 1 hour.

7 *To serve* (15 minutes): Whip
the cream until thick, then use
to decorate the flan with the
reserved raspberries. Cut the flan
into large wedges.

Menu Suggestion
This pretty dessert is good for a
dinner party because it can be
made completely the day before.
Serve Chilled Ratatouille
(page 22) to start, and Pork with
Cider and Coriander (page 36) for
the main course.

BAKED RUM AND RAISIN CHEESECAKE

1.40* 🍴 £ £ ✳ 452 cals

* plus 1 hour cooling

Serves 8

75 g (3 oz) raisins
75 ml (5 tbsp) dark rum
225 g (8 oz) self-raising flour
5 ml (1 tsp) bicarbonate of soda
5 ml (1 tsp) cream of tartar
75 g (3 oz) butter
rind of 1 lemon
150 ml ($\frac{1}{4}$ pint) soured cream
125 g (4 oz) cottage cheese
125 g (4 oz) full-fat soft cheese
2 eggs, separated
50 g (2 oz) caster sugar
150 ml ($\frac{1}{4}$ pint) double cream
15 ml (1 tbsp) icing sugar, to decorate

1 *To prepare* (1 hour 35 minutes): Put the raisins and rum in a saucepan and bring to the boil. Turn off the heat and leave to cool for 15 minutes.

2 Meanwhile, sift the flour into a bowl with the bicarbonate of soda and cream of tartar. Rub in the butter.

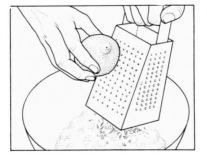

3 Grate in the lemon rind, using the finest side of the grater. Bind to a smooth dough with the soured cream, then use to line a greased 25 cm (10 inch) flan dish.

4 In a bowl, beat together the cottage and cream cheeses. Stir in the rum and raisins.

5 In a separate bowl, whisk the egg yolks and caster sugar until pale and fluffy. Whisk in the double cream, and continue whisking until the mixture is the consistency of lightly whipped cream. Fold into the cheese, rum and raisin mixture.

6 Whisk the egg whites until stiff and fold into the mixture. Pour it into the prepared pastry case and bake in the oven at 180°C (350°F) mark 4 for about 1 hour. Turn off the heat and leave to cool in the oven for 15 minutes. Remove from the oven and cool for a further 45 minutes.

7 *To serve* (5 minutes): Cut into slices and dust with icing sugar.

Menu Suggestion
Serve this traditional, rich cheesecake after a light main course such as grilled steak, chops or Marinated Lamb Cutlets (page 30).

FRUIT AND NUT CRUMBLE

| 1.05 | £ ✳* | 410 cals |

* freeze at the end of step 4

Serves 4

100 g (4 oz) plain wholewheat flour

pinch of salt

50 g (2 oz) butter or margarine

100 g (4 oz) demerara sugar

25 g (1 oz) walnuts, finely chopped

3 cooking pears

1 large cooking apple

30 ml (2 tbsp) redcurrant jelly

finely grated rind and juice of
    1 lemon

1 To prepare (25 minutes): Mix the flour and salt in a bowl. Add the butter or margarine and rub in until the mixture resembles fine breadcrumbs. Stir in half the sugar and the walnuts. Set aside.

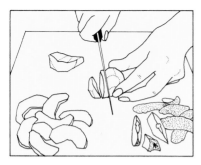

2 Peel and quarter the pears and apple. Remove the cores, then slice the flesh thinly.

3 In a bowl, mix the redcurrant jelly and the lemon rind and juice with the remaining sugar. Add the sliced fruit and fold gently to mix.

4 Turn the fruit into an oven-proof dish and sprinkle the crumble mixture over the top. Leave in a cool place or the refrigerator until ready to cook (overnight if convenient).

5 To serve (40 minutes): Bake in the oven at 180°C (350°F) mark 4 for 40 minutes or until the fruit feels soft when pierced with a skewer and the crumble topping is crisp and golden. Serve hot.

Menu Suggestion
This nutty pear and apple crumble is a filling family pudding. Serve with pouring cream, custard or ice cream.

SHERRIED APRICOT TRIFLE

| 1.00* | 🍴 | 573 cals |

* plus cooling, setting and overnight chilling

Serves 8–10

410 g (14½ oz) can apricot halves in natural juice

127 g (4½ oz) packet orange- or tangerine-flavoured jelly

350 g (12 oz) Madeira cake

300 ml (½ pint) sherry

1 egg

2 egg yolks

25 g (1 oz) caster sugar

15 ml (1 tbsp) cornflour

450 ml (¾ pint) milk

300 ml (½ pint) double or whipping cream

few strips of angelica and some glacé cherries, to decorate

1 *To prepare* (45 minutes): Drain the apricots and measure the juice. Make up the jelly according to packet instructions, using the apricot juice as part of the measured liquid. Leave in a cool place until cold and just beginning to set.

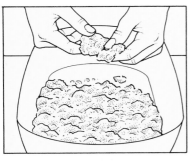

2 Meanwhile break up the cake with your fingers and place in the bottom of a glass serving dish. Pour over the sherry, place the apricots on top, reserving one for decoration, cover and leave to stand while making the custard.

3 Make the custard. Put the egg and egg yolks in a bowl with the sugar and whisk lightly together. Add the cornflour and a few tablespoons of the milk and whisk again until combined.

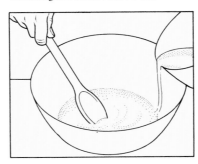

4 Scald the milk in a heavy-based saucepan. Pour on to the egg mixture, stirring constantly, then return the custard to the rinsed-out pan. Cook over low to moderate heat, stirring all the time until the custard thickens and coats the back of the spoon. Pour immediately into a bowl, cover the surface of the custard closely with cling film and leave until cold.

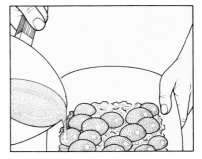

5 Pour the cold, setting jelly over the apricots in the serving dish, spreading it evenly, then chill in the refrigerator until set.

6 Pour the cold custard over the jelly, cover closely with cling film and chill overnight.

7 *To serve* (15 minutes): Whip the cream until stiff, then swirl or pipe over the trifle leaving the centre uncovered. Decorate with the remaining apricot, angelica 'stalks', and glacé cherry 'flowers'. Serve chilled.

Menu Suggestion
A special occasion trifle, which can be served as a dessert for a buffet party, or as a teatime treat.

SHERRIED APRICOT TRIFLE
Trifle is an old-fashioned English dish, traditionally served at Sunday tea time. Every English family has its own version, but the authentic English trifle which was so popular in Victorian days was a simple layered concoction of Madeira cake soaked in sherry, almond-flavoured macaroons or ratafias, a rich egg custard and a topping of thickly whipped cream. Today's modern trifle with fruit and jelly would have been frowned upon by the Victorians.

The essence of making a good trifle lies in using a large quantity of sherry for soaking the Madeira cake base. It may seem extravagant when you are making it, but unless you use the amount specified in the recipe, you will not get the proper 'boozy' flavour, which is vital to a really good special-occasion trifle like this.

POMMES BRISTOL

| 0.45* | 🏺 | £ | 303 cals |

* plus cooling and overnight chilling
Serves 4

225 g (8 oz) sugar

450 ml (¾ pint) water

1 vanilla pod

4 crisp dessert apples (e.g. Granny Smiths or Cox's Orange Pippin)

2 small oranges

30 ml (2 tbsp) orange-flavoured liqueur (optional)

1 To prepare (40 minutes): Put half the sugar in a heavy-based saucepan with 300 ml (½ pint) of the water and the vanilla pod. Heat gently until the sugar has dissolved, then simmer, without stirring, for 2–3 minutes.

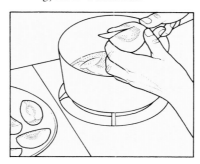

2 Meanwhile, peel, quarter and core the apples. Slice them into the pan of syrup, remove from the heat and cover with a lid.

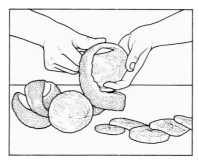

3 Cut the rind and pith off the oranges with a serrated knife, working from top to bottom in a spiral motion. Slice into thin rounds or sections.

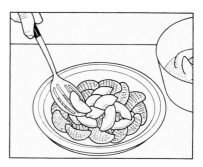

4 When the apples are cold, remove them carefully from the syrup with a slotted spoon. Arrange them on a shallow serving dish with the orange. Discard the vanilla pod from the syrup and stir in the liqueur, if using. Pour over the apples and oranges, cover with cling film and chill in the refrigerator overnight.

5 Put the remaining sugar and water in the saucepan and heat gently until the sugar has dissolved. Boil rapidly until the syrup turns a rich caramel in colour, then pour immediately into a greased shallow baking tin or tray. Leave in a cold place overnight.

6 To serve (5 minutes): Crush the caramel into small pieces by hitting it with the end of a rolling pin or a mallet. Sprinkle over the apples and oranges and serve immediately (the caramel will soften if left on the fruit and syrup for many minutes).

Menu Suggestion
Serve this fruity dessert after a rich main course.

MANGO MOUSSE

`1.00*` ⬧ £ £ `375 cals`

* plus 15 minutes freezing or 1 hour chilling, and overnight refrigeration

Serves 6

2 ripe mangoes

3 eggs

1 egg yolk

40 g (1½ oz) caster sugar

finely grated rind of 1 orange

60 ml (4 tbsp) orange-flavoured liqueur or orange juice

300 ml (½ pint) double cream

15 ml (1 tbsp) powdered gelatine

30 ml (2 tbsp) lemon juice

30 ml (2 tbsp) water

shreds of blanched orange rind, to decorate

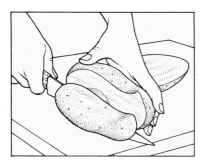

1 *To prepare* (50 minutes): Cut a thick slice from either side of each central mango stone, keeping the knife close to the stone.

2 Scrape the mango flesh out of the skin and from around the stone. Place in a blender or food processor and work to a smooth purée, then rub through a nylon sieve into a bowl. Set aside.

3 With an electric mixer, beat the eggs, egg yolk and sugar in a separate bowl until thick and light in colour. The beaters should leave a ribbon trail on the surface.

4 Add the mango purée. Whisk in the orange rind and the liqueur or orange juice to the egg mixture a little at a time, whisking well after each addition.

5 Whip half the cream until it is the same consistency as the mango mousse, then fold in.

6 Sprinkle the gelatine over the lemon juice and water in a small heatproof bowl. Leave for 5 minutes until spongy, then stand the bowl in a pan of gently simmering water to dissolve.

7 Pour the liquid gelatine into the mango mousse, stirring gently to distribute it evenly. Pour slowly into a chilled large serving dish. Freeze for 15 minutes or chill for 1 hour. Cover with cling film and chill overnight.

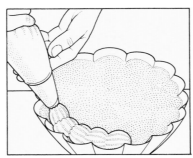

8 *To serve* (10 minutes): Whip the remaining cream until stiff, then use to pipe a shell border around the edge of the mousse. Sprinkle with orange shreds. Serve chilled.

Menu Suggestion

Mango Mousse is a very special dinner party dessert. Serve it after Beef Kabobs with Horseradish Relish (page 35) or Pork with Cider and Coriander (page 36).

COFFEE BAVARIAN CREAM

| $1.45*$ | 🍳 | £ £ | 555 cals |

* plus 3 hours or overnight chilling

Serves 6

125 g (4 oz) roasted coffee beans

900 ml (1½ pints) milk

6 egg yolks

75 g (3 oz) caster sugar

20 ml (4 tsp) powdered gelatine

60 ml (4 tbsp) water

300 ml (½ pint) double cream

30 ml (2 tbsp) coffee-flavoured liqueur

coffee dragees and coarsely grated chocolate, to decorate

1 *To prepare* (1 hour 30 minutes): Put the coffee beans in a saucepan and place over low heat for 2–3 minutes, shaking the pan frequently. Off the heat, pour all the milk into the pan, then return to the heat and bring to the boil. Remove from the heat, cover the pan and leave to infuse for at least 30 minutes.

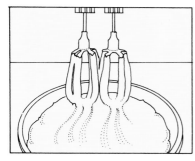

2 Beat the egg yolks and caster sugar in a bowl until thick and light in colour. The beaters should leave a ribbon trail on the surface of the mixture when lifted.

3 Strain on the milk and stir well. Pour into the rinsed out pan and stir over low heat for 10 minutes. Do *not* boil. Strain into a large bowl; cool for 20 minutes.

4 Sprinkle the gelatine over the water in a small heatproof bowl. Leave for 5 minutes until spongy, then stand the bowl in a pan of gently simmering water and heat until dissolved.

5 Stir the gelatine into the custard. Stand this in a roasting tin of cold water and ice cubes. Stir until the mixture is cool and about to set.

6 Lightly whip half of the cream to the thick pouring stage, then fold into the custard. Pour into a lightly oiled 1.4 litre (2 pint) moule-à-manqué cake tin or soufflé dish. Chill for at least 3 hours or overnight until completely set.

7 *To serve* (15 minutes): With dampened fingers, gently ease the edges of the cream away from the tin. Turn the cream out on to a flat plate, shaking the tin or dish gently until the cream moves and loosens inside the tin. Carefully ease off the tin and slide the cream into the centre of the plate.

8 Whip the remaining cream until stiff, then gradually whisk in the coffee liqueur. Spoon into a piping bag fitted with a 1 cm (½ inch) star nozzle and pipe rosettes around the top edge of the cream. Decorate with coffee dragees and grated chocolate. Serve chilled.

Menu Suggestion

A classic dinner party dessert, Coffee Bavarian Cream would go well after a main course of Marinated Lamb Cutlets (page 30). Serve Nutty Camembert Pâté (page 13) to start.

BLACKBERRY ICE CREAM

| 0.40* | 🍴 £ ✳ | 436 cals |

* plus 1 hour cooling, 9 hours
freezing and 2 hours softening

Serves 6

**450 g (1 lb) blackberries, fresh or
frozen**

30 ml (2 tbsp) thick honey

50 g (2 oz) caster sugar

**410 g (14½ oz) can evaporated milk,
chilled**

150 ml (¼ pint) double cream

**30 ml (2 tbsp) orange-flavoured
liqueur**

45 ml (3 tbsp) lemon juice

**single cream and wafer biscuits,
to serve**

1 To prepare (35 minutes): Pick
over fresh blackberries, wash
and drain well. Place the berries
in a small saucepan with the
honey and sugar, cover the pan
and cook gently for 5–10 minutes
until soft.

2 Purée in a blender or food
processor, then pass through a
nylon sieve to remove pips. Leave
to cool for about 1 hour.

3 Whip the evaporated milk
until it thickens slightly, then
whisk the cream to the same
consistency and fold gently
together. Stir in the fruit purée
with the liqueur and lemon juice.

4 Pour into a container (not
metal). Freeze for about 3
hours or until set to a mushy
consistency.

5 Remove from the freezer and
beat well to break down the ice
crystals. Return to the freezer for
at least 6 hours.

6 To serve (5 minutes): Allow the
ice cream to 'come to' in the
refrigerator for 2 hours. Scoop
into individual glass dishes and
serve with single cream and wafer
biscuits.

Menu Suggestion

This is a sophisticated ice cream
containing orange-flavoured
liqueur. Serve for a dinner party
dessert after a light main course.

ICED ORANGE SABAYON

0.25* | £ £ | ✳ | 282 cals

* plus 30 minutes cooling and 3–4 hours freezing

Serves 6

6 egg yolks

175 g (6 oz) demerara sugar

90 ml (6 tbsp) orange-flavoured liqueur

200 ml (7 fl oz) unsweetened orange juice

glacé cherries and candied peel, to decorate

1 To prepare (20 minutes): Put the egg yolks and sugar in a bowl and beat together until pale and creamy. Stir in the liqueur and orange juice.

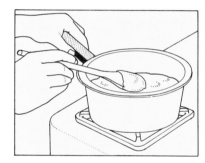

2 Pour into a medium-sized heavy-based saucepan. Stir over low heat until the mixture thickens and just coats the back of the spoon. Do *not* boil.

3 Pour into 6 individual soufflé dishes or ramekins and cool for at least 30 minutes. Freeze for 3–4 hours until firm. Wrap in cling film and return to the freezer.

4 To serve (5 minutes): Serve straight from the freezer, decorated with cherries and peel.

Menu Suggestion

Iced Orange Sabayon makes a good dessert to serve after a rich main course such as Creamed Seafood Vol-au-Vents (page 51).

Baking

Cakes and other bakes can be cooked ahead of time whenever you've time to spare, so that when the unexpected visitor calls there is always something delicious and homemade to offer. Why not plan a cook-ahead baking session one rainy day? Choose a few of the recipes in this chapter and plan to make them all at the same time. This makes economic use of oven space, saves on fuel bills and will stand you in good stead for future entertaining.

ORANGE MADEIRA CAKE

| 1.40* | £ | ✳ | 534 cals |

* plus 1 hour cooling and 1 day storing

Serves 6

175 g (6 oz) butter

175 g (6 oz) caster sugar

3 eggs, beaten

150 g (5 oz) self-raising flour

100 g (4 oz) plain flour

finely grated rind of 1 orange and 30 ml (2 tbsp) juice

25 g (1 oz) cube sugar

4 Fold in the grated orange rind with the orange juice. Spoon the mixture into the prepared tin. Smooth the surface with a palette knife.

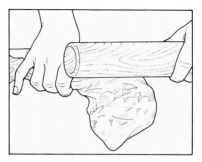

5 In a strong polythene bag, crush the cube sugar, then sprinkle it evenly over the cake surface.

6 Bake in the oven at 170°C (325°F) mark 3 for about $1\frac{1}{4}$ hours, or until firm to the touch. Turn out on to a wire rack, place the right way up and leave to cool for 1 hour. Store for at least 1 day before serving.

7 *To serve* (5 minutes): Cut into 12 slices.

Menu Suggestion

This is a plain cake with a tangy bite to it. Serve sliced at teatime, or cut in thin wedges with Madeira or port after dinner.

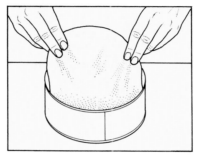

1 *To prepare* (1 hour 35 minutes): Grease and base line an 18 cm (7 inch) round deep cake tin.

2 Put the butter or margarine and caster sugar in a bowl and beat together until light and fluffy.

3 Gradually beat in the eggs. Sift the plain and self-raising flours into the bowl, then fold in with a large metal spoon.

ORANGE MADEIRA CAKE

Madeira cake is well worth making at home because it has a much lighter texture and a more buttery flavour than commercial varieties. It is one of England's most famous cakes, which gained popularity in the 19th century, when it was the tradition to offer a slice of cake and a glass of Madeira wine to morning callers.

FRUIT BRAZIL CAKE

| 0.45* | 🍴 | £ £ ✳ | 700–933 cals |

* plus 1 hour 10 minutes cooling

Serves 6–8

175 g (6 oz) butter or block margarine

175 g (6 oz) caster sugar

3 eggs, size 2, beaten

125 g (4 oz) Brazil nuts

50 g (2 oz) candied lemon peel

125 g (4 oz) dried apricots

125 g (4 oz) sultanas

125 g (4 oz) plain flour

125 g (4 oz) self-raising flour

2 tablespoons apricot jam, sieved and melted

225 g (8 oz) marzipan and a few Brazil nuts, to decorate

1 *To prepare* (30 minutes): Line the bottom and sides of a 20.5 cm (8 inch) round cake tin or a 1.7 litre (3 pint) loaf tin with greased greaseproof paper.

2 Put the butter and sugar in a bowl and cream together until light and fluffy. Gradually beat in the eggs.

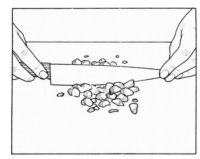

3 Chop or coarsely grate the nuts. Finely chop the candied peel. Snip the apricots into small pieces. Mix all the fruit and nuts together.

4 Sift the flours together and fold into the creamed mixture followed by the fruit mixture. Spoon into the prepared tin.

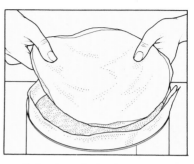

5 Bake the cake in the oven at 180°C (350°F) mark 4 for about 1¼ hours. Cool for 10 minutes in the tin, then turn out on to a wire rack for 1 hour.

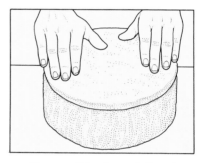

6 *To serve* (15 minutes): Brush the top of the cake with the apricot jam. Roll out the marzipan to fit the cake; press on top.

7 Crimp the edges and score the top in a diamond pattern. Decorate with the Brazil nuts. Grill the cake to brown the top. Store for up to 1 week.

Menu Suggestion

Serve Fruit Brazil Cake instead of a traditional Christmas Cake.

APPLE PARKIN

| 2.05* | £ | ✳ | 632–766 cals |

* plus 2 hours cooling and 2 days storing

Serves 6–8

450 g (1 lb) eating apples
25 g (1 oz) butter or margarine
225 g (8 oz) plain flour
10 ml (2 tsp) baking powder
15 ml (3 tsp) ground ginger
50 g (2 oz) lard
125 g (4 oz) medium oatmeal
75 g (3 oz) caster sugar
125 g (4 oz) golden syrup
125 g (4 oz) black treacle
1 egg, beaten
30 ml (2 tbsp) milk
Cheddar cheese wedges, to serve

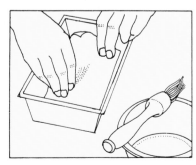

1 *To prepare* (2 hours): Grease and base line a 1.7 litre (3 pint) loaf tin.

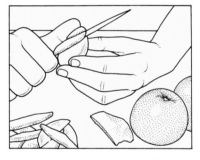

2 Peel, quarter, core and chop the apples. Melt the butter in a small saucepan, add the apples, cover and cook gently until soft. Beat the apples to a purée, then cool for about 1 hour.

3 Sift the flour, baking powder and ginger into a large bowl. Rub in the lard; stir in the oatmeal and sugar.

4 Warm the syrup and treacle together until evenly mixed, then stir into the dry ingredients with the apple purée, egg and milk. Stir until evenly blended.

5 Turn into the prepared tin and bake in the oven at 180°C (350°F) mark 4 for about 1½ hours, covering loosely with foil after 45 minutes.

6 Turn out of the tin and cool on a wire rack for 1 hour. Wrap and store for 2 days before eating.

7 *To serve* (5 minutes): Slice and accompany with wedges of Cheddar cheese.

Menu Suggestion

Yorkshire parkin is traditionally eaten with cheese, and the apples in this version go particularly well with it. Try it with a sharp Cheddar or Wensleydale for an unusual packed lunch.

FRUITY GINGERBREAD

| 1.05* | £ | ✳ | 164 cals |

* plus cooling and 3 days maturing

Makes about 20 squares

| 75 g (3 oz) butter or margarine |
| 100 g (4 oz) dark soft brown sugar |
| 100 g (4 oz) golden syrup |
| 100 g (4 oz) black treacle |
| 225 g (8 oz) medium oatmeal |
| 100 g (4 oz) self-raising flour |
| 50 g (2 oz) mixed dried fruit |
| 10 ml (2 tsp) ground ginger |
| pinch of salt |
| 175 ml (6 fl oz) milk |
| butter for spreading (optional) |

1 *To prepare* (1 hour): Melt the butter or margarine in a saucepan with the sugar, syrup and treacle.

2 Meanwhile, in a bowl, mix together the oatmeal, flour, fruit, ginger and salt.

3 Pour the melted mixture into the bowl, then the milk. Beat vigorously with a wooden spoon until all the ingredients are evenly combined.

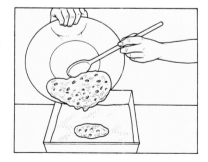

4 Pour the mixture into a greased and base-lined 25 cm (10 inch) square baking tin. Bake in the oven at 180°C (350°F) mark 4 for 45 minutes or until firm to the touch.

5 Allow to cool in the tin for 10 minutes, then turn out on to a wire rack and leave until cold. Wrap in cling film or foil and store in an airtight tin for 3 days until the gingerbread is really moist.

6 *To serve* (5 minutes): Unwrap and cut into about 20 squares. Spread with butter if liked.

Menu Suggestion
This moist gingerbread, with its added fruit, is bound to be popular with children. Pop a slice or two in the school packed lunch box.

ICED MARZIPAN ROUNDS

| 1.10* | ☐ | £ £ | ✳* | 235 cals |

* plus 1 hour chilling, 30 minutes cooling and 30 minutes drying; freeze at the end of step 7

Makes 8

| 100 g (3½ oz) plain flour |
| 40 g (1½ oz) caster sugar |
| 40 g (1½ oz) butter or margarine |
| 1 egg yolk |
| 75 g (3 oz) yellow-coloured marzipan |
| 25 ml (5 tsp) dark rum |
| 30 ml (2 tbsp) apricot jam |
| 100 g (4 oz) icing sugar |
| yellow food colouring |

1 *To prepare* (1 hour 10 minutes): Mix the flour and caster sugar together in a bowl. Add the butter or margarine and rub in with the fingertips. Mix to a smooth dough with the egg yolk and 5 ml (1 tsp) water.

2 Turn the dough out on to a floured surface and knead lightly until smooth. Wrap and chill in the refrigerator for 30 minutes.

3 On a floured surface, roll the dough out to a 3 mm (⅛ inch) thickness. With a 5 cm (2 inch) round fluted cutter, stamp out 16 rounds. Prick with a fork.

4 Place the rounds on lightly greased baking sheets, then chill again in the refrigerator for 30 minutes.

5 Bake in the oven at 180°C (350°F) mark 4 for about 20 minutes. Transfer to a wire rack and leave to cool for 30 minutes.

6 Knead the marzipan with a few drops of the rum. Lightly dust the work surface with a little icing sugar, then roll the marzipan out to a 3 mm (⅛ inch) thickness. With the same 5 cm (2 inch) cutter, stamp out 8 rounds.

7 Brush each cooled biscuit with a little melted apricot jam. Sandwich together with a marzipan round in the centre.

8 Beat the icing sugar and remaining rum together. Divide in half. Add a few drops of colouring to one half.

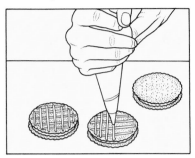

9 Using small piping bags and plain nozzles, lattice the rounds with icing. Leave to dry for at least 30 minutes.

10 *To serve*: Serve immediately, or store in a single layer in airtight containers for up to 5 days.

Menu Suggestion

Make these unusual sandwich biscuits for a special teatime treat. The children will love the marzipan and apricot jam filling, and the different coloured icings make the biscuits really eye-catching.

ICED MARZIPAN ROUNDS

Marzipan is another name for almond paste, made from sugar, almonds and egg white. The origins of marzipan are uncertain. Some say it was introduced to Europe by the Arabs, others that it was created by a French order of nuns. Literally translated, the word marzipan means 'St Mark's bread', and European cuisines have a fair number of marzipan specialities connected with religious festivals. Sicily and Germany, for example, have marzipan fruits and vegetables at Christmas, whereas England has simnel cake at Easter and iced cakes with marzipan are served for Christmas and other celebrations. Marzipan can be either yellow or white.

LEMON AND LIME COOKIES

0.55* £ ✳* 91 cals

* plus 30 minutes cooling; freeze after cooling in step 4

Makes 24

100 g (4 oz) butter or margarine
100 g (4 oz) caster sugar
1 egg yolk
50 g (2 oz) full-fat soft cheese
175 g (6 oz) plain flour
finely grated rind of 1 small lemon
15 ml (1 tbsp) lemon juice
20 ml (4 tsp) lime marmalade

1 *To prepare* (40 minutes): Put the butter or margarine and caster sugar in a bowl and beat together until light and fluffy.

2 Beat in the egg yolk, cheese, flour, lemon rind and juice, until a soft mixture is formed.

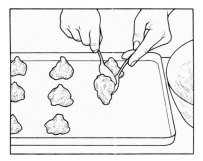

3 Place small spoonfuls of the mixture on to greased baking sheets, allowing room for spreading.

4 Bake in the oven at 190°C (375°F) mark 5 for about 17 minutes or until light brown. Transfer to a wire rack to cool for at least 30 minutes. Store in an airtight container for up to 3 days.

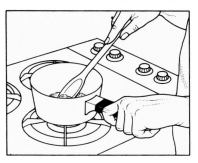

5 *To serve* (15 minutes): Melt the marmalade in a small saucepan and brush over the cookies, to glaze. Leave to set for 5 minutes before serving.

Menu Suggestion
With their tangy marmalade glaze, these cookies taste good at any time of day, but they go particularly well with morning coffee.

LEMON AND LIME COOKIES

These cookies are simplicity itself to make, almost like craggy, flat rock cakes. If you have a food processor, steps 1 and 2 can be made in moments, by working all the ingredients together in one go.

You will find the flavours of lemon and lime together are just perfect with a morning cup of coffee, but children may find the lime a little too tangy. You can of course use ordinary orange marmalade for the glaze if you wish, together with the finely grated rind of 1 small orange and 15 ml (1 tbsp) orange juice, instead of the lemon in the recipe. This makes the cookies quite a bit sweeter.

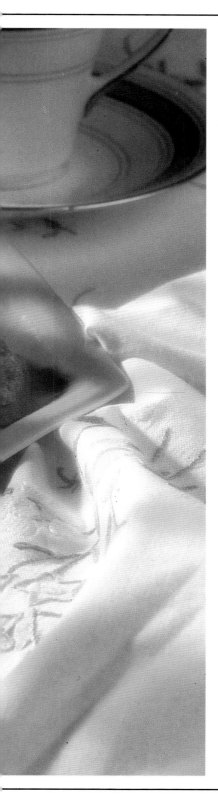

ZIGZAG BATON

1.25*	🍞 £	1869 cals

* plus 24 hours rising, 1 hour at room
temperature and 1 hour proving

Makes one 450 g (1 lb) loaf

about 300 ml (½ pint) milk and
    water, mixed
5 ml (1 tsp) sugar
7.5 ml (1½ tsp) dried yeast
225 g (8 oz) plain wholewheat flour
225 g (8 oz) strong plain white flour
10 ml (2 tsp) salt
25 g (1 oz) butter
beaten egg, to glaze
poppy seeds, to decorate

1 *To prepare* (35 minutes):
Warm the milk and water to
lukewarm. Pour half into a bowl
and stir in the sugar until
dissolved.

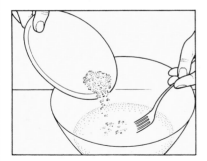

2 Sprinkle in the yeast, whisk
with a fork, then leave to stand
in a warm place for 10–15 minutes
until frothy.

3 Mix the flours and salt in a
warmed large bowl. Rub in the
butter with the fingertips.

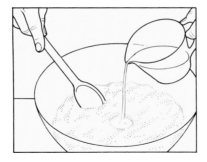

4 Make a well in the centre, add
the yeast and the remaining
milk and water and mix with a
wooden spoon. If too dry, add a
little more lukewarm water.

5 Turn the dough on to a
floured surface and knead for
10 minutes until smooth and
elastic. Place in a lightly oiled
polythene bag and leave to rise in
the refrigerator for 24 hours.

6 *To serve* (50 minutes): Remove
the risen dough from the
refrigerator and allow to come to
room temperature for 1 hour.
Turn on to a floured surface and
knead for 2–3 minutes to break
down any air bubbles.

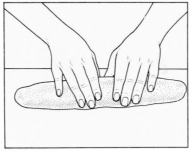

7 Using both hands, roll the
dough into a sausage shape,
about 40.5 cm (16 inches) long.
Place on a greased baking sheet.

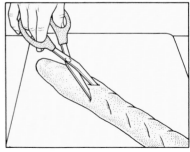

8 With a pair of sharp scissors
held at a 30° angle to the top
surface of the dough, make V-
shaped cuts about three-quarters
of the way through it at 5 cm
(2 inch) intervals.

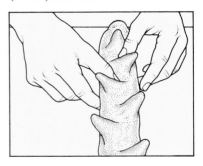

9 Pull each section of dough out
to alternate sides to give a
'zigzag' appearance. Leave to
prove in a warm place for about 1
hour or until doubled in bulk.

10 Brush the dough with
beaten egg, then sprinkle
with poppy seeds. Bake in the
oven at 230°C (450°F) mark 8 for
30 minutes until golden. Cool on a
wire rack before serving.

Menu Suggestion
Serve this unusually shaped loaf
just as you would ordinary bread.
Made with half wholewheat and
half white flour, it has an
interesting texture and flavour.

Fork Supper

A simple fork supper is perfect for informal entertaining—say after the theatre or a concert. This menu serves 8, but it can be easily adjusted for more or less. The Lamb and Mushroom au Gratin, a pasta dish like cannelloni, with a lamb, mushroom and tomato filling, can be made up to 1–2 days in advance, as can the Fresh Pineapple Compote. Simply pop the gratin dish in the oven and put the final decorations on the pineapple while your guests are having pre-supper drinks.

LAMB AND MUSHROOM AU GRATIN

2.00* ⬚ £ ✳* 566 cals

* plus 10 minutes cooling; freeze at
the end of step 5

Serves 8

65 g (2½ oz) butter

700 g (1½ lb) mushrooms, finely
   chopped

15 ml (1 tbsp) vegetable oil

700 g (1½ lb) lean minced lamb

1 garlic clove, skinned and
   crushed

227 g (8 oz) can tomatoes, drained

75 g (3 oz) plain flour

15 ml (1 tbsp) chopped fresh
   oregano or 5 ml (1 tsp) dried

15 ml (1 tbsp) chopped fresh
   rosemary or 5 ml (1 tsp) dried

150 ml (¼ pint) dry white wine

salt and freshly ground pepper

16 sheets cooked lasagne, about
   275 g (10 oz) raw weight

900 ml (1½ pints) milk

100 g (4 oz) Cheddar cheese, grated

100 g (4 oz) Mozzarella cheese,
   grated or finely chopped

1 *To prepare* (1 hour 15 minutes):
Melt 25 g (1 oz) of the butter
in a large saucepan, add the
mushrooms and cook over
moderate heat for about 10
minutes until soft and reduced in
volume.

2 Heat the oil in a large frying
pan, add the lamb and brown
well; drain off all the fat. Stir in
the garlic, mushrooms, tomatoes,
30 ml (2 tbsp) of the flour and the
herbs. Cook for 1–2 minutes, then
add the wine and seasoning to
taste. Bring to the boil, then
simmer for about 30 minutes,
uncovered. Cool for 10 minutes.

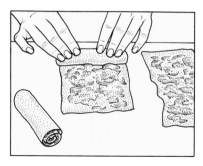

3 Spread the mixture over the
sheets of lasagne and roll up
each sheet from one short side.

4 Cut the rolls into three. Pack
tightly together, standing
upright, in one large or two small
5 cm (2 inch) deep straight-sided
ovenproof dishes.

5 Melt the remaining butter in a
saucepan, add the remaining
flour and cook over low heat,
stirring with a wooden spoon, for
2 minutes. Gradually blend in the
milk, stirring after each addition
to prevent lumps forming. Bring
to the boil slowly, then simmer for
2–3 minutes, stirring. Add plenty
of seasoning then pour over the
pasta. Leave to cool, then cover
and chill in the refrigerator until
required.

6 *To serve* (45 minutes): Bake in
the oven at 200°C (400°F)
mark 6 for about 40 minutes.
Uncover, sprinkle with the cheeses
and grill until golden. Serve hot.

FRESH PINEAPPLE COMPOTE

0.50* 🥘 £ £ 114 cals

* plus overnight chilling

Serves 8

2 small ripe pineapples

60 ml (4 tbsp) orange-flavoured liqueur

567 g (1 lb 4 oz) can lychees in syrup

shelled pistachio nuts, to decorate

1 To prepare (35 minutes): Cut each pineapple lengthways into quarters, slicing through the 'crown' at the top. Cut out the hard central cores and discard.

2 Using a serrated knife, carefully cut all around the edge of each pineapple 'boat' between the flesh and the skin.

3 Carefully work the knife underneath the pineapple flesh, to release it completely from the skin. Cut the flesh into bite-sized cubes. Wrap the pineapple shells in cling film and set aside.

4 Put the pineapple cubes in a bowl and sprinkle over the liqueur. Drain the lychees, pouring the syrup into a saucepan. Add three-quarters of the lychees to the pineapple.

5 Boil the lychee syrup until reduced by half, then leave to cool. Add to the pineapple and lychees and fold gently to mix. Cover the bowl with cling film and chill overnight, with the pineapple shells and reserved lychees.

6 To serve (15 minutes): Cut the reserved lychees into flower shapes. Divide the pineapple and lychees equally between the 8 shells and pour over the syrup. Decorate with the lychee 'flowers' and pistachios. Serve chilled.

FRESH PINEAPPLE COMPOTE

Canned lychees are available at most good supermarkets. They have a deliciously sweet flavour and unusual texture, and can be used in fruit salads of all kinds to add a touch of exotic interest. Lychees (also called lichees and litchis) are native to China, but they also grow in India and South Africa. The fresh fruit are available at some specialist markets and greengrocers in late summer, but they are not easy to recognise if you are only familiar with the canned fruit. The skin of fresh lychees is rough and brittle, almost like a bark.

Cold Lunch Party

For summer entertaining in the garden, nothing could be more relaxing than a cold lunch party — especially when all the preparations can be done beforehand. Salmon in Puff Pastry makes a spectacular table centre-piece, and the two salad accompaniments complement each other perfectly. All you need to serve with them is plenty of crusty French bread and butter, and a selection of cheeses. Finish with the Open Pear Flan, and your guests will be amazed how perfect the food is, with no sign of cooking!

SALMON IN PUFF PASTRY

| 1.45* | £ £ ✳* | 583–640 cals |

* plus 30 minutes chilling, 1 hour
cooling and 30 minutes at room
temperature

Serves 6

1 bunch watercress
45 ml (3 tbsp) soured cream
finely grated rind of ½ lemon
salt and freshly ground pepper
1.1–1.4 kg (2½–3 lb) salmon or sea trout, cleaned and filleted (see box)
1 quantity puff pastry (see page 157) or two 368 g (13 oz) packets frozen puff pastry, thawed
beaten egg, to glaze

1 *To prepare* (1 hour 10 minutes): Wash the watercress and trim off the root ends. Chop roughly, then place in a bowl with the soured cream. Add the lemon rind and seasoning to taste, then stir until the ingredients are well mixed.

2 Using a sharp knife and holding the tail end of 1 salmon fillet, scrape the flesh away from the skin. Repeat with the other fillets.

3 Place two fillets skinned side down on a board and spoon on the prepared watercress filling. Top with the remaining fillets.

4 If using frozen pastry, stack one piece on top of the other. Roll out the home-made or frozen pastry to a rectangle about 30 × 23 cm (12 × 9 inches).

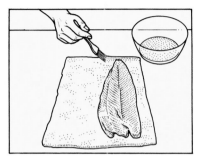

5 Carefully place the fish on the pastry, leaving a 5 mm (¼ inch) border. Brush the edges of the pastry with beaten egg.

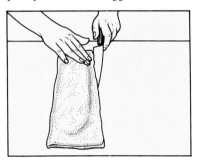

6 Fold the pastry over the fish to enclose it completely. Seal and trim, then knock up the edges. Lift on to a baking sheet and chill in the refrigerator for at least 30 minutes.

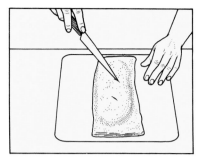

7 Use the remaining egg to glaze the pastry. Make 2 small holes in the pastry to allow the steam to escape. Place the baking sheet in the oven and bake at 200°C (400°F) mark 6 for about 45 minutes until the pastry is well risen and golden brown. To test, make a small slit through the thickest part of the fish —the flesh should begin to flake. Cool for at least 1 hour then wrap in cling film or foil and refrigerate for up to one day.

8 *To serve* (35 minutes): Remove the salmon from the refrigerator and unwrap. Leave at room temperature for 30 minutes before serving.

SALMON IN PUFF PASTRY

Your fishmonger will clean the salmon for you, but to get four neat fillets, you may prefer to fillet it yourself. Cut off the head and tail and snip off the fins. Rinse the fish and pat dry. Place on a board, head end towards you, and snip along the belly from head to tail. Starting with the flesh nearest to the belly, ease the flesh away from the bones, using a filleting knife and short sharp strokes. Open out the fish and slide the knife tip under the end of the exposed bone. Using a similar action as before, work along the length of the fish to remove the bone completely. Pluck out any small bones in the flesh. Snip the skin between the halves to give two fillets, then neaten the edges. Repeat the process with the other fillet.

FENNEL WITH GREEN PEPPERCORN DRESSING

| **1.00*** | £ | 103 cals |

* plus 20 minutes cooling

Serves 6

3 heads of fennel
salt and freshly ground pepper
15–30 ml (1–2 tbsp) lemon juice
150 ml ($\frac{1}{4}$ pint) whipping cream
15 ml (1 tbsp) green peppercorns
10 ml (2 tsp) white wine or
tarragon vinegar

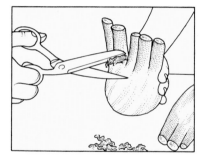

1 To prepare (50 minutes): Trim any green leafy tops from the fennel and reserve. Cook the fennel in plenty of boiling salted water to which the lemon juice has been added, for 30–35 minutes or until just tender.

2 Drain well, then rinse immediately under cold running water. Cool completely; about 20 minutes. Cover and chill.

3 Lightly whip the cream. Roughly crush or chop the peppercorns, then fold them into the cream with the vinegar and seasoning to taste. Cover and chill.

4 To serve (10 minutes): Split the fennel heads in half and place on a flat serving dish. Spoon over the peppercorn dressing and garnish with the reserved snipped fennel tops.

PASTA AND ANCHOVY SALAD WITH GARLIC DRESSING

| 0.55* | 406 cals |

* plus at least 2 hours or overnight standing

Serves 6

two 50 g (2 oz) cans anchovies in oil

45 ml (3 tbsp) milk

350 g (12 oz) small pasta shapes (see box)

salt and freshly ground pepper

1 garlic clove, skinned and roughly chopped

75 ml (3 fl oz) vegetable oil

juice of $\frac{1}{2}$ lemon

185 g (6$\frac{1}{2}$ oz) can pimientos, drained

60 ml (4 tbsp) mayonnaise

1 To prepare (45 minutes): Drain the anchovies, place in a bowl and add the milk. Leave to soak for 30 minutes (this helps remove excess salt).

2 Meanwhile, cook the pasta in plenty of boiling salted water according to the packet instructions until *al dente* (tender but firm to the bite).

3 Drain the anchovies and rinse under cold running water. Pat dry with absorbent kitchen paper.

4 Reserve a few of the anchovies whole for garnishing and crush the remainder to a paste with the garlic. Add the oil and lemon juice gradually, whisking with a fork until thick. Add pepper to taste.

5 Drain the pasta and turn into a large bowl. Pour in the dressing immediately and toss well to mix. Leave to cool, then cover and chill in the refrigerator for at least 2 hours, or overnight if more convenient.

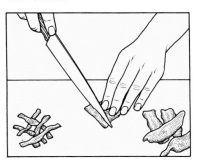

6 To serve (10 minutes): Cut the pimiento into thin strips. Add to the pasta salad, reserving a few for garnish. Add the mayonnaise and toss gently to mix. Taste and adjust seasoning. Pile the salad into a serving bowl and arrange the remaining whole anchovies and pimiento strips in a lattice pattern over the top. Serve at room temperature.

PASTA AND ANCHOVY SALAD WITH GARLIC DRESSING

Supermarkets and delicatessens now stock a huge variety of different pasta shapes, which make interesting salads as well as the more usual hot pasta dishes which are served with a sauce. For salads, don't buy the very tiny pasta shapes—these are only for use in soups. Choose small shapes such as *conchiglie* (seashells), which are excellent for trapping salad dressings and preventing ingredients sinking to the bottom of the salad bowl. *Fusilli* (spirals) and *farfalle* (bow ties) can also be used.

OPEN PEAR FLAN

| 1.20* | ☐ | £ £ | ✳* | 464 cals |

* plus 1 hour cooling; freeze at the end of step 6

Serves 6

1½ quantities pâte sucrée (see page 158)

50 g (2 oz) butter

50 g (2 oz) caster sugar

1 egg, size 6, beaten

50 g (2 oz) ground almonds

20 ml (4 tsp) plain flour

10 ml (2 tsp) pear- or almond-flavoured liqueur

3 ripe pears (Conference, William or Packham)

100 g (4 oz) apricot jam

30 ml (2 tbsp) water

1 *To prepare* (1 hour 10 minutes): Roll out the pâte sucrée on a lightly floured work surface and use to line a 25 cm (10 inch) loose-bottomed fluted flan ring. Prick the bottom with a fork and chill in the refrigerator for at least 15 minutes.

2 Meanwhile, put the butter and sugar in a bowl and beat together until light and fluffy. Beat in the egg and stir in the ground almonds, flour and liqueur. Pour into the pastry case and level the surface.

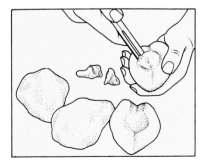

3 Carefully peel the pears, cut them in half lengthways, and remove the core with a melon baller or teaspoon.

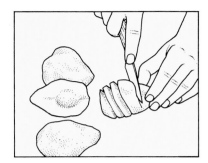

4 Lay each pear half cut side down, and cut them crossways into thin slices. Keeping each pear half intact, place on the almond mixture to form the spokes of a wheel, then press each half slightly to fan out the pear slices.

5 Bake in the oven at 200°C (400°F) mark 6 for 10–15 minutes until the pastry just begins to brown. Turn the oven temperature down to 180°C (350°F) mark 4 and bake for a further 20–25 minutes.

6 Remove from the oven and cool for 1 hour. Store in an airtight container for not longer than 1 day.

7 *To serve* (10 minutes): Place the jam in a saucepan and add the water. Heat gently, stirring until the jam softens. Bring to the boil and simmer for 1 minute. Sieve and brush over the flan while still warm.

Midweek Party

Entertaining in the middle of the week can be a problem especially if you're out at work all day. With this simple three-course menu, everything can be prepared the night before, just leaving last-minute touches and soufflé-making before your guests arrive.

AUBERGINE AND CHEESE SOUFFLÉ

| 1.25 | 🍳 f | 454 cals |

Serves 4

450 g (1 lb) aubergines

salt and freshly ground pepper

75 g (3 oz) butter

30 ml (2 tbsp) plain flour

150 ml ($\frac{1}{4}$ pint) milk

100 g (4 oz) Red Leicester or Cheddar cheese, grated

4 eggs, separated

40 g ($1\frac{1}{2}$ oz) freshly grated Parmesan cheese

1 *To prepare* (45 minutes): Chop the aubergines roughly and place in a colander or sieve. Sprinkle liberally with salt and set aside to drain for 30 minutes. Rinse under cold running water, then pat dry with absorbent kitchen paper.

2 Melt 50 g (2 oz) of the butter in a saucepan, add the aubergines, cover and cook gently until golden brown and completely soft. Purée in a blender or food processor until nearly smooth.

3 Melt the remaining butter in a clean saucepan, add the flour and cook over low heat, stirring with a wooden spoon, for 2 minutes. Remove the pan from the heat and gradually blend in the milk, stirring after each addition to prevent lumps forming. Bring to the boil slowly, then simmer for 2–3 minutes, stirring.

4 Remove from the heat and stir in the aubergine purée, the Red Leicester or Cheddar cheese, the egg yolks and seasoning to taste. Turn into a bowl, cover and chill in the refrigerator until required.

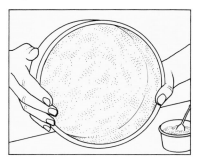

5 *To serve* (40 minutes): Lightly grease a 1.4 litre ($2\frac{1}{2}$ pint) soufflé dish and dust out with all but 25 g (1 oz) of the Parmesan cheese.

6 Whisk the egg whites until stiff but not dry. Fold into the aubergine mixture until evenly combined. Spoon into the prepared dish and sprinkle with the remaining Parmesan. Bake in the oven at 200°C (400°F) mark 6 for 25–30 minutes. Serve immediately.

AUBERGINE AND CHEESE SOUFFLÉ

Making a soufflé is much easier than you think. Not only are soufflés quick, and therefore perfect for midweek entertaining, they are also ideal for making the night before and finishing off just before your guests arrive. Most savoury soufflés have a simple base of thick béchamel sauce, to which chopped or puréed vegetables are added, often with a flavouring of cheese, as in this recipe. The secret of successful soufflé making lies at the end of the preparation. The egg whites must be stiffly whisked and then quickly folded into the thick sauce with a large metal spoon — to incorporate as much air as possible. Serve at once, before the soufflé starts to subside.

HUNGARIAN PORK

2.45* £ £ ✳* 770 cals

* plus overnight chilling; freeze at the
end of step 7

Serves 4

700 g (1½ lb) pork shoulder

1 medium onion, skinned and
  roughly chopped

1 large garlic clove, skinned and
  roughly chopped

50 g (2 oz) stuffed green olives

100 g (4 oz) fresh white
  breadcrumbs

salt and freshly ground pepper

1 egg, beaten

30 ml (2 tbsp) flour

700 g (1½ lb) fresh spinach,
  trimmed and washed (see box)

1.25 ml (¼ tsp) grated nutmeg

50 g (2 oz) butter

450 g (1 lb) ripe tomatoes, skinned
  and sliced

30 ml (2 tbsp) vegetable oil

200 ml (7 fl oz) chicken stock

200 ml (7 fl oz) dry white wine

7.5 ml (1½ tsp) paprika

150 ml (¼ pint) soured cream

extra paprika, to garnish

1 To prepare (1 hour 30 minutes):
Trim the fat off the pork, then
put through the mincer twice with
the onion, garlic and olives. Turn
into a bowl, add the breadcrumbs
and seasoning to taste and mix
well. Bind with the beaten egg.

2 With floured hands, roll the
mixture into 36 small balls.
Coat in the remaining flour, then
chill for 30 minutes.

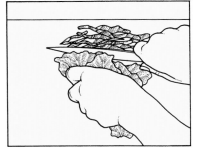

3 Meanwhile cook the spinach
in a large saucepan with only
the water that clings to the leaves.
Drain well, then chop finely. Add
the nutmeg and seasoning to taste.

4 Melt half the butter in a large
frying pan, add the tomatoes
and fry for 1–2 minutes. Transfer
to an ovenproof casserole. Place
the spinach on top.

5 Melt the remaining butter
with the oil in the frying pan,
add the meatballs in batches and
fry over moderate heat until
lightly coloured on all sides.
Remove from the pan with a
slotted spoon and drain on
absorbent kitchen paper.

6 Add the stock and wine to the
frying pan and bring to the
boil, stirring to scrape up the
sediment from the base and sides
of the pan. Add the paprika and
seasoning to taste, then remove
from the heat. Cool for 5 minutes,
then stir in 45 ml (3 tbsp) of the
soured cream.

7 Put the meatballs on top of the
spinach in the casserole, then
pour over the sauce. Leave until
cold, then cover and chill
overnight.

8 To serve (1 hour 15 minutes):
Cook in the oven at 200°C
(400°F) mark 6 for 1¼ hours.
Serve hot straight from the
casserole or transfer to a serving
dish. Drizzle with the remaining
soured cream and the extra
paprika.

HUNGARIAN PORK

It is not always possible to
buy fresh spinach exactly when
you want it, but frozen spinach
can be used in this recipe with
almost equal success. If you can,
buy the frozen whole leaf
spinach, as it tends to have
more body than the chopped
varieties. To make up the
equivalent of 700 g (1½ lb) fresh
spinach for this recipe, you will
need 350–450 g (12 oz–1 lb)
frozen. Thaw the spinach in step
3 by heating it gently in a heavy
saucepan for about 10 minutes,
stirring and breaking up any
lumps with a spoon. If using leaf
spinach, do not chop it or it will
go too limp.

INDIVIDUAL PEACH MERINGUES

| 3.10* | ❊* | 319 cals |

* plus cooling time; freeze meringue nests after cooling in step 4

Serves 4

2 egg whites, size 2

pinch of salt or cream of tartar

50 g (2 oz) granulated sugar

50 g (2 oz) caster sugar

350 g (12 oz) frozen raspberries

50 g (2 oz) icing sugar

60 ml (4 tbsp) kirsch

2 ripe peaches

150 ml ($\frac{1}{4}$ pint) single cream

1 *To prepare* (2–2$\frac{1}{2}$ hours): Line a baking sheet with foil or non-stick baking parchment.

2 Put the egg whites in a bowl with the salt or cream of tartar. Whisk until very stiff. Add half of the granulated and caster sugar a little at a time, whisking after each addition until stiff peaks form. Fold in the remaining sugar lightly with a large metal spoon.

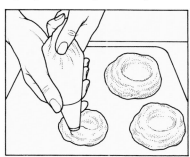

3 Fill a piping bag fitted with a large star nozzle and pipe the meringue into 4 'nests' on the lined baking sheet.

4 Dry out the meringues in the oven at 130°C (250°F) Gas mark $\frac{1}{2}$ for about 2 hours until they are firm and crisp. Transfer carefully from the baking sheet to a wire rack and leave until cold. Store in an airtight tin for up to 1 week.

5 *To serve* (40 minutes): Put the raspberries in a bowl and sprinkle with the icing sugar and kirsch. Leave to macerate for about 30 minutes, folding gently to mix once the raspberries start to thaw.

6 Meanwhile, skin the peaches and halve and stone them. Cut the flesh into neat slices.

7 Spoon the raspberries into the meringue cases, then arrange the peach slices on top. Serve immediately, or the meringues will become soft. Hand the cream separately.

INDIVIDUAL PEACH MERINGUES

It isn't absolutely necessary to pipe these meringues, although it is very simple, and it does make them look extra special for a dinner party. If you haven't got a piping bag and nozzle, simply spoon 4 heaps of meringue on to the lined baking sheet and hollow out the centres with the back of the spoon, to make rough 'nest' shapes. The meringue will hold its shape during baking exactly as it does when piped. If your meringues begin to brown too much during the baking time, simply prop open the oven door a little.

Portable Picnic

If you're planning a picnic, you want to be able to get up and go, especially if the weather promises to be good. All the recipes in this picnic menu keep and travel well, so you can make them and pack them ready the night before.

FRIED SALAMI CHICKEN

0.45* | 593 cals

* plus 1 hour cooling time

Serves 6

12 chicken drumsticks, skinned

**24 slices of salami, skinned
(about 100 g [4 oz])**

3 eggs, size 2, beaten

450 g (1 lb) fresh breadcrumbs

vegetable oil for deep frying

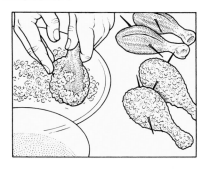

3 Dip the salami-filled chicken first into beaten egg, then breadcrumbs and pat the crumbs in well. Repeat the egg and bread-crumb process to give a good coating.

4 Heat the oil in a deep-fat fryer to 180°C (350°F) and fry the chicken for 7–10 minutes, until golden brown and cooked through. Drain on absorbent kitchen paper and leave to cool for about 1 hour.

5 *To serve* (5 minutes): Carefully remove the cocktail sticks from the drumsticks before packing.

1 *To prepare* (45 minutes): Make an incision to the bone along 1 side of each chicken drumstick and loosen the flesh around the bone.

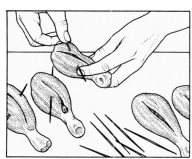

2 Place 2 slices of salami around the bone, pull the chicken flesh together and secure with cocktail sticks.

FRIED SALAMI CHICKEN

Virtually any salami can be used for this recipe, but it is best to avoid the fatty Danish salami, which is easily recognisable by its bright pink appearance. Instead, choose a good Italian salami such as Genova or Napoli. Hungarian salamis are also good, as is Cervelat, which is a partially dried sausage rather than a true salami.

ASPARAGUS AND BACON QUICHE

| 1.15* | 619 cals |

* plus 1 hour cooling, and chilling

Serves 6

700 g (1½ lb) fresh asparagus spears (about 24), or 225 g (8 oz) frozen

225 g (8 oz) plain flour

125 g (4 oz) butter or margarine

about 60 ml (4 tbsp) ice-cold water

125 g (4 oz) thinly sliced streaky bacon, rinded

4 egg yolks

450 ml (¾ pint) single cream

100 g (4 oz) Gruyère cheese, grated

salt and freshly ground pepper

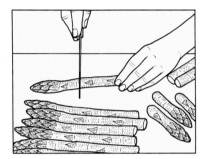

1 To prepare (1 hour 10 minutes): Trim the heads off fresh asparagus to the length of about 4 cm (1½ inches). (Use the stalks for soup.) Blanch the heads in boiling salted water for 5 minutes; drain. If using frozen asparagus, cook in boiling water for 5 minutes then drain and trim as above.

2 Put the flour in a bowl, add the butter and rub in with the fingertips until the mixture resembles fine breadcrumbs. Add enough ice-cold water to bind to a firm dough.

3 Turn the dough out on to a floured surface and roll out to fit a 25 cm (10 inch) fluted flan dish. Bake blind in the oven at 190°C (375°F) mark 5 for 15 minutes until set but not browned.

4 Meanwhile, with a knife, stretch the bacon rashers on a flat surface. Wrap a small piece around each asparagus head.

5 In a bowl, mix the egg yolks with the cream, grated cheese and seasoning to taste. Spoon into the flan case.

6 Arrange the asparagus and bacon rolls in the custard. Reduce the oven temperature to 180°C (350°F) mark 4 and bake for 30–35 minutes or until set and golden brown. Cool for 1 hour, then wrap in cling film and store in the refrigerator until required (but not longer than 2 days).

7 To serve (5 minutes): Cut into wedges.

ASPARAGUS AND BACON QUICHE

To make a quick asparagus soup with the stalks not used in this recipe: chop the stalks and cook them in butter with a little finely chopped onion. Add 1.1 litres (2 pints) chicken stock, the finely grated rind and juice of ½ a lemon and salt and pepper to taste. Simmer for about 20 minutes until all the asparagus is tender, then purée in a blender or food processor. Reheat with 150 ml (¼ pint) single cream before serving.

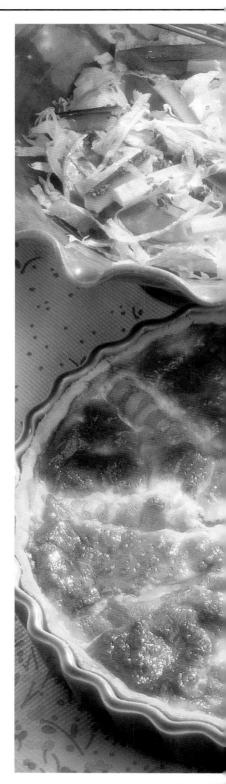

MANGE-TOUT SALAD

0.20* £ 155 cals

* plus 30 minutes cooling

Serves 6

225 g (8 oz) mange-touts, trimmed

salt and freshly ground pepper

30 ml (2 tbsp) vegetable oil

1 cucumber

30 ml (2 tbsp) single cream

45 ml (3 tbsp) French dressing (see page 155)

chopped fresh parsley and mint

1 To prepare (15 minutes): Cook the mange-touts in boiling salted water for about 4 minutes; drain and return to the pan. While still hot, add the oil and toss until well coated. Leave to cool for at least 30 minutes, then cover and chill in the refrigerator until required.

2 Cut the cucumber into 5 cm (2 inch) sticks, add to the mange-touts, cover with cling film and chill in the refrigerator until required.

3 Whisk the cream and French dressing together with the parsley and mint, pour into a screw-topped jar and chill in the refrigerator until required.

4 To serve (5 minutes): Place the mange-touts and cucumber in a salad bowl. Shake the dressing once more, pour over the vegetables and serve immediately.

POTTED CHEESE WITH MINT

0.20*	£	✳	409 cals

* plus at least 2 hours chilling

Serves 6

75 g (3 oz) butter, at room temperature

225 g (8 oz) Red Leicester or Cheddar cheese

15 ml (1 tbsp) chopped fresh mint

60 ml (4 tbsp) soured cream

freshly ground pepper

mint leaves, to garnish

brown bread or crispbreads, to serve

1 *To prepare* (15 minutes): Put the butter in a bowl and beat until really soft. Grate in the cheese, then beat it gradually into the butter.

2 Stir in the chopped mint and soured cream, adding freshly ground pepper to taste. (Salt should not be required as the cheese contains sufficient.)

3 Spoon into 4–6 individual serving dishes and garnish with mint leaves. Cover with cling film and chill in the refrigerator for at least 2 hours.

4 *To serve* (5 minutes): Spread on slices of brown bread or crispbreads.

POTTED CHEESE WITH MINT

The English semi–hard Red Leicester is excellent for making potted cheese because of its interesting orange-red colour. It also has the right kind of flaky texture which blends smoothly and makes it easy to spread. Red Leicester is also a good melting cheese, so try it in cooking instead of Cheddar.

SPICED APPLE TORTE

| 1.20* | £ | ✳ | 627 cals |

* plus 1 hour cooling

Serves 6

| 175 g (6 oz) butter or margarine |
| 175 g (6 oz) light soft brown sugar |
| 75 g (3 oz) oat flakes |
| 5 ml (1 tsp) ground cinnamon |
| 450 g (1 lb) cooking apples |
| finely grated rind of 1 lemon |
| 45 ml (3 tbsp) lemon juice |
| 2 eggs, beaten |
| 125 g (4 oz) self-raising flour |
| 5 ml (1 tsp) ground mixed spice |
| 300 ml (½ pint) single cream, to serve |

1 To prepare (75 minutes): Melt 50 g (2 oz) of the butter or margarine in a saucepan. Add 50 g (2 oz) of the sugar and the oats and cinnamon and fry gently, stirring, until golden.

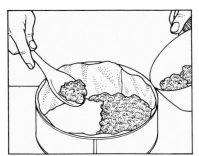

2 Spoon the mixture into a greased and lined 19 cm (7½ inch) round cake tin.

3 Peel and core the apples, then slice them thinly into a bowl. Stir in the lemon rind and juice. Set aside.

4 Put the remaining butter or margarine in a separate bowl, add the remaining sugar and beat together until light and fluffy. Beat in the eggs gradually. Sift in the flour with the spice and stir in, followed by the apple mixture.

5 Spoon the mixture into the cake tin and level the surface. Bake in the oven at 180°C (350°F) mark 4 for about 50 minutes. Turn out on to a baking sheet lined with non-stick paper. Cool completely: about 1 hour. Cover and chill until required or for up to 2 days.

6 To serve (5 minutes): Unwrap, cut into wedges and serve with single cream.

SPICED APPLE TORTE

This cake tastes equally delicious with orange flavouring, so you can ring the changes each time you make it—which is bound to be often! Substitute the finely grated rind of 1 medium orange for the lemon rind, and the same quantity of freshly squeezed orange juice as specified for lemon in the recipe.

At the end of the summer when there are plenty of fresh pears about, you can use cooking pears such as Conference, instead of the apples. Pears taste best with lemon, but you may prefer to use ground ginger rather than cinnamon, since ginger and pears have a special affinity for one another.

ENTERTAINING FRIENDS AT THE WEEKEND

Saturday Lunch

Friends or relations arriving Saturday lunchtime and staying over until Sunday tea? Make it a relaxed weekend with these suggested menus, all of which can be prepared in the days leading up to the Saturday, thus leaving you free to enjoy the company of your guests. Start with an elegant seafood and French bean salad for Saturday lunch, followed by homemade bread rolls and cheese. First impressions count!

SEAFOOD IN SAFFRON MAYONNAISE

0.55 £ £ 493 cals

Serves 6

450 g (1 lb) white fish fillets
    (haddock, cod or monkfish)

1 bay leaf

1 slice lemon

125 g (4 oz) peeled prawns

125 g (4 oz) cooked, shelled
    mussels

few saffron threads

1 egg yolk

150 ml ($\frac{1}{4}$ pint) vegetable oil

10 ml (2 tsp) white wine vinegar

salt and freshly ground pepper

450 g (1 lb) French beans, topped,
    tailed and cooked

chopped fresh parsley, to garnish

1 *To prepare* (45 minutes): Place the fish in a large frying pan, cover with water and add the bay leaf and lemon slice. Bring to the boil, then immediately lower the heat and poach gently for 10–15 minutes until cooked. Strain off the poaching liquid, reserving 60 ml (4 tbsp). Cool the fish for at least 20 minutes.

2 Skin the fish and roughly flake the flesh. Place in a bowl with the prawns and mussels, cover and chill for up to 2 days.

3 Meanwhile put the reserved fish liquor in a small saucepan, add the saffron threads and heat gently. Remove from the heat and leave to infuse until cold and golden yellow in colour.

4 Put the egg yolk in a bowl and beat well. Beat in the oil a drop at a time, then continue adding in a thin, steady stream until the mixture is very thick. Stir in half the vinegar and continue beating in the oil until all is incorporated. Stir in the remaining vinegar.

5 Strain the saffron liquid into the mayonnaise and whisk to the consistency of single cream. Add seasoning to taste, cover and chill in the refrigerator for up to 2 days.

6 *To serve* (10 minutes): Arrange the French beans on a long serving dish. Pile the fish mixture down the centre of the beans and spoon over the mayonnaise. Serve immediately, garnished with parsley.

SEAFOOD IN SAFFRON MAYONNAISE

Most good fishmongers sell monkfish, and if you can get it for this recipe, then you will find it better for a special occasion than cod or haddock. Although more expensive, its flavour is rather like that of lobster, and its flesh is very thick, firm and white—again like lobster, or scampi. Monkfish hasn't always been such a highly prized fish. Because of its unattractive appearance when whole, it used to be unpopular, but once the head is removed and the fish cut into fillets by the fishmonger, you need never know how ugly it was! In some areas it is known as angler fish or frog fish, and if you have eaten it in Mediterranean countries you will probably know it by either its Spanish name of *rape*, or by the French name *lotte* or *ange de mer*, or the Italian *rospo* (which means frog).

QUICK WHOLEMEAL ROLLS

0.35*	£	✳	149 cals

*plus 1 hour rising

Makes 12

15 g (½ oz) fresh yeast or 7.5 ml (1½ tsp) dried

10 ml (2 tsp) sugar

300 ml (½ pint) tepid water

225 g (8 oz) strong white flour

225 g (8 oz) strong wholewheat flour

10 ml (2 tsp) salt

15 g (½ oz) lard

cracked wheat, to decorate

1 *To prepare* (35 minutes): Grease a baking sheet. Blend the fresh yeast, 5 ml (1 tsp) sugar and the water. If using dried yeast, dissolve 5 ml (1 tsp) sugar in the water, sprinkle in the yeast and leave to froth for 15 minutes.

2 Sift the flours into a bowl with the salt and 5 ml (1 tsp) sugar. Rub in the fat. Add the yeast mixture and mix to a soft dough. Turn on to a lightly floured surface and knead for about 2 minutes until smooth.

3 Divide the dough into 12 equal pieces and shape into rounds. Place on the greased baking sheet, brush with water and sprinkle the tops with cracked wheat. Cover with a clean damp tea cloth and leave to rise in a warm place for about 1 hour until doubled in size.

4 Bake at 230°C (450°F) mark 8 for 15–20 minutes or until golden brown. Cool for at least 15 minutes on a wire rack.

GARLIC AND BLACK PEPPERCORN CHEESE

| 0.45* | £ | ✳ | 113 cals |

*plus 2½–4 days draining and chilling
Makes 450 g (1 lb)

600 ml (1 pint) single cream
568 ml (1 pint) milk
30 ml (2 tbsp) buttermilk
1 garlic clove, skinned
5 ml (1 tsp) salt
15 ml (1 tbsp) chopped fresh mixed herbs (parsley, chervil, chives, thyme)
30 ml (2 tbsp) black peppercorns, coarsely crushed
cucumber slices, to garnish

1 *To prepare* (35 minutes): Put the cream and milk in a saucepan and heat gently to blood heat or 32–38°C (90–100°F); stir in the buttermilk. Pour the mixture into a bowl.

2 Cover the bowl with cling film and leave in a warm place for 24–48 hours until the cream mixture turns to soft curds.

3 Line a colander with muslin or all-purpose kitchen cloth and place it in the sink. Pour the curds into the colander and drain for 10 minutes.

4 Place the colander on a rack in a saucepan, cover with cling film and chill in the refrigerator for 18–24 hours.

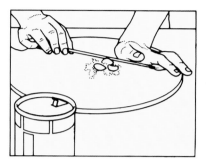

5 On a board, crush the garlic to a smooth purée with the flat of a round-bladed knife and the salt. Spoon the curds from the colander into a bowl and stir in the mixed herbs, garlic and peppercorns.

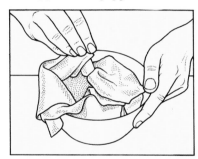

6 Line a small plastic punnet or earthenware cheese mould with a double layer of damp cheesecloth or all-purpose kitchen cloth, leaving a 5 cm (2 inch) overhang. Spoon in the curds and fold the cheesecloth over the top.

7 Invert the punnet or mould on to a wire rack placed over a shallow dish, cover tightly with cling film and chill for 18–24 hours.

8 *To serve* (10 minutes): Unmould the cheese on to a plate, remove the cheesecloth and garnish with cucumber slices. Serve chilled.

Saturday Dinner

This should be the high spot of the weekend. If you've planned not to eat out, then your menu at home should match that of the best restaurant in town! Start with a refreshingly tangy Avocado and Orange Salad with Citrus Dressing. Follow with a rich veal dish with wine, mushrooms and cream, which both looks and tastes very special, and yet is incredibly simple to prepare. Then finish the meal with Iced Strawberry Soufflé — a spectacular finale to any meal.

Avocado and Orange Salad with Citrus Dressing

*0.40**	462 cals

* plus 1 hour or overnight chilling

Serves 6

150 ml ($\frac{1}{4}$ pint) vegetable oil

105 ml (7 tbsp) freshly squeezed grapefruit juice

15 ml (1 tbsp) snipped chives

2.5 ml ($\frac{1}{2}$ tsp) sugar

salt and freshly ground pepper

3 medium oranges

3 ripe avocados

1 To prepare (25 minutes): Put the oil in a screw-top jar with the grapefruit juice, chives, sugar and seasoning to taste. Shake well to mix.

2 Working in a spiral motion, remove the rind and white pith from the oranges with a serrated knife.

3 Cut the oranges into segments and place in a shallow dish. Shake the dressing again, then pour over the oranges. Cover the dish with cling film and chill in the refrigerator for at least 1 hour, or for up to 24 hours if more convenient.

4 To serve (15 minutes): Cut the avocados in half and twist to remove the stones. Peel off the skin, then slice the flesh neatly.

5 Remove the orange segments from the marinade and arrange on individual plates, alternating with avocado slices. Pour over the marinade and serve immediately.

VEAL ESCALOPES WITH CREAM AND MUSHROOM SAUCE

| 0.55* | 445 cals |

* plus cooling and chilling

Serves 6

6 veal escalopes, about 100 g (4 oz) each

30 ml (2 tbsp) plain flour

salt and freshly ground pepper

50 g (2 oz) butter

30 ml (2 tbsp) olive oil

350 g (12 oz) button mushrooms, sliced

350 ml (12 fl oz) dry white wine

10 ml (2 tsp) chopped fresh tarragon or 5 ml (1 tsp) dried

200 ml (7 fl oz) double cream

tarragon sprigs, to garnish

1 To prepare (35 minutes): Trim each veal escalope to remove any skin, then cut each one in half.

2 Place the escalopes well apart between sheets of non-stick paper or heavy-duty cling film. Bat out well, using a meat mallet or rolling pin, until the escalopes are very thin. Remove paper or film, then coat the escalopes in the flour seasoned with salt and pepper.

3 Melt the butter with the oil in a heavy-based frying pan. Add the escalopes a few at a time and fry over moderate heat until lightly coloured on both sides. Remove with a spatula and set aside on a plate.

4 Add the mushrooms to the pan and fry until the juices run. Add the wine and bring slowly to the boil, stirring, then return the escalopes to the pan, pile the mushrooms on top and sprinkle with the tarragon and seasoning to taste. Turn into a shallow dish. Leave to cool, then cover and refrigerate until ready to serve (overnight, if convenient).

5 To serve (20 minutes): Cook over moderate heat and bring slowly to the boil. Lower the heat, cover and simmer for 5–10 minutes until heated through. Remove the veal from the cooking liquid with a slotted spoon, arrange in a warmed serving dish and keep hot. Stir the cream into the pan and simmer until the sauce thickens. Taste and adjust seasoning, then pour over the veal. Serve immediately, garnished with sprigs of tarragon.

VEAL ESCALOPES WITH CREAM AND MUSHROOM SAUCE

Although veal is an expensive meat to buy, escalopes work out less so because they are beaten very thin and therefore weigh very little.

Escalopes come from the leg of the calf. The topside is the choicest cut, from which come the most tender escalopes. Slightly less expensive but still good are the escalopes from the thick flank. Some butchers sell escalopes cut from the 'skirt' of the animal. These have a good flavour, but they do have a coarse grain which makes it necessary to cook them longer. Check with your butcher when buying so you can be sure of the cooking time.

ICED STRAWBERRY SOUFFLÉ

| 3.05* | 🍴 | £ £ | ❄ | 569 cals |

* plus 1–2 hours setting, 3 hours freezing, 2 hours softening

Serves 6

225 g (8 oz) strawberries

60 ml (4 tbsp) almond-flavoured liqueur

30 ml (2 tbsp) lemon juice

15 ml (1 tbsp) icing sugar

300 ml ($\frac{1}{2}$ pint) double cream

45 ml (3 tbsp) water

15 ml (1 tbsp) powdered gelatine

4 eggs, separated

175 g (6 oz) caster sugar

225 g (8 oz) strawberries

25 g (1 oz) small ratafias or macaroons

150 ml ($\frac{1}{4}$ pint) double cream

1 *To prepare* (1 hour): Put the strawberries in a bowl and stir in the liqueur, lemon juice and icing sugar. Cover and leave to marinate for 30 minutes.

2 Put the strawberries in a blender or food processor and work to a purée. Sieve to remove the seeds.

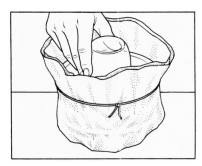

3 Tie a double band of grease-proof paper around the edge of a 1.1 litre (2 pint) soufflé dish to form a 5 cm (2 inch) collar. Stand a straight-sided 450 g (1 lb) jam jar in the centre.

4 Lightly whip the 300 ml ($\frac{1}{2}$ pint) of cream until it just holds its shape.

5 Put the water into a small saucepan, sprinkle over the gelatine and leave to soak for about 5 minutes until spongy. Dissolve slowly over gentle heat.

6 Put the egg yolks and caster sugar in a bowl and whisk with an electric whisk until very light and creamy. Fold in the strawberry purée, whipped cream and dissolved gelatine.

7 Whisk the egg whites until stiff but not dry and fold into the strawberry mixture.

8 Pour the mixture into the prepared dish, keeping the jam jar in the centre. Chill in the refrigerator for 1–2 hours until set, then transfer to the freezer for at least 3 hours, until firm.

9 *To serve* (2 hours 5 minutes): Remove the soufflé from the freezer and fill the jam jar with hot water. Twist gently to remove it. Fill the centre with the straw-berries. Finely crush the ratafias or macaroons. Ease off the paper collar and coat the sides of the soufflé with crushed ratafias. Decorate with the cream, whipped.

10 Transfer to the main body of the refrigerator for about 2 hours to soften before serving.

Sunday Brunch and Tea

Get off to a late, leisurely start on Sunday morning. Make a pot of fresh coffee to wake everyone up, then crack open a bottle of Champagne—and treat your guests to the sumptuous sensation of fresh salmon. Before they leave, there's a special teatime treat—the fabulous French savarin, a ring of sweet yeast cake soaked in rum. Served with a medley of fresh fruits and cream, nothing could round off the weekend better.

FRESH SALMON KEDGEREE

0.45*	£ £	378 cals

* plus cooling

Serves 6

350 g (12 oz) fresh salmon

150 ml (¼ pint) dry white wine

2 small onions, skinned and chopped

1 carrot, peeled and sliced

1 celery stick, trimmed and chopped

15 ml (1 tbsp) lemon juice

6 peppercorns

1 bouquet garni

salt and freshly ground pepper

275 g (12 oz) long-grain rice

50 g (2 oz) butter

7.5 ml (1½ tsp) English mustard powder

3 hard-boiled eggs, shelled and quartered

cayenne pepper, to finish

celery leaves, to garnish

1 *To prepare* (10–15 minutes):
Put the salmon in a saucepan, pour in the wine and enough water to cover the fish. Add half of the chopped onions, the carrot, celery, lemon juice, peppercorns, bouquet garni and 5 ml (1 tsp) salt.

2 Bring slowly to the boil, then immediately remove from the heat. Cover the pan tightly with a lid and leave to cool. Chill in the refrigerator for up to 48 hours.

3 *To serve* (25–30 minutes):
Cook the rice in plenty of boiling salted water for 15–20 minutes until tender.

4 Meanwhile, remove the salmon from the liquid and flake the flesh, discarding skin and any bones. Strain the cooking liquid and reserve.

5 Melt half of the butter in a large frying pan, add the remaining onion and fry gently until soft. Drain the rice thoroughly, then add to the onion with the remaining butter. Toss gently to coat in the butter and stir in the mustard powder.

6 Add the flaked salmon and the hard-boiled eggs and a few spoonfuls of the strained cooking liquid to moisten. Heat through. Shake the pan and toss the ingredients gently so that the salmon and eggs do not break up. Transfer to a warmed serving dish and sprinkle with cayenne to taste. Serve immediately, garnished with celery leaves.

FRESH SALMON KEDGEREE

Kedgeree, sometimes also called khichri, is a rice dish of Anglo-Indian origin. In the days of the Raj it was very popular for breakfast, made with smoked fish rather than the fresh salmon used here. Original recipes for kedgeree are made with curry powder or curry spices and the rice can be quite hot and spicy, but the delicate flavour of fresh salmon would be overpowered by pungent spices, so they are not used here.

Fresh salmon is a luxury, but for weekend guests it is well worth the expense. Look for salmon trout and farm trout, which are cheaper than the freshwater salmon.

FRUIT AND RUM SAVARIN

1.40* 🔲 £ £ ✳* 568 cals

* plus rising, proving and cooling;
freeze savarin only, at the end of
step 7

Serves 6

15 g ($\frac{1}{2}$ oz) fresh yeast

45 ml (3 tablespoons) lukewarm
    milk

100 g (4 oz) strong plain flour,
    sifted with a pinch of salt

30 ml (2 tbsp) caster sugar

2 eggs, beaten

50 g (2 oz) unsalted butter, softened

225 g (8 oz) granulated sugar

200 ml (7 fl oz) water

120 ml (8 tbsp) dark rum

2 bananas, peeled and sliced

450 g (1 lb) black grapes, halved
    and seeded

2 kiwi fruit, peeled and sliced

2 small oranges, skinned and
    segmented

single cream, to serve

1 *To prepare* (1 hour 30 minutes):
Put the yeast in a warmed
small bowl and add the milk;
cream together. Add 25 g (1 oz) of
the flour and beat well with a fork.
Leave in a warm place for 10–15
minutes until frothy.

2 Put the remaining flour in a
warmed large bowl with 5 ml
(1 tsp) of the caster sugar and the
eggs. Add the frothy yeast
mixture, then beat until an elastic
dough is formed. Cover with a
floured tea towel and leave in a
warm place until doubled in size.

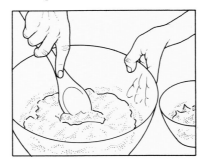

3 Beat the softened butter into
the dough a little at a time
until all is evenly incorporated.

4 Put the dough in a buttered
and floured 1.1 litre (2 pint)
savarin or ring mould. Cover with
a floured tea towel and leave to
prove in a warm place until it has
risen to the top of the mould.

5 Uncover the mould and bake
the savarin in the oven at
200°C (400°F) mark 6 for 25–30
minutes until risen and golden
brown.

6 Meanwhile, make the rum
sugar syrup. Put the granulated sugar and water in a heavy-
based saucepan and heat gently
until the sugar has dissolved.
Bring to the boil and boil steadily,
without stirring, for 5 minutes
until syrupy. Remove from the
heat and stir in 90 ml (6 tbsp) of
the rum.

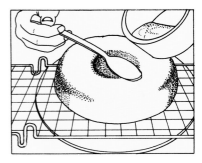

7 Turn the savarin out on to a
wire rack placed over a large
plate or tray. Prick all over the
savarin with a fine skewer, then
slowly spoon over the warm syrup.
Collect any syrup that drips on to
the plate or tray and spoon it back
over the savarin. Leave until completely cold. Transfer to an
airtight tin until required (up to 48
hours).

8 *To serve* (10 minutes): Toss
the prepared fruits together
with the remaining caster sugar
and rum. Place the savarin on a
serving plate and pile the fruits in
the centre. Serve immediately
with chilled single cream.

USEFUL INFORMATION
AND
BASIC RECIPES

Useful Hints

Planning your kitchen well and making full use of today's selection of labour-saving gadgets enables you to prepare and cook meals ahead of time, with the minimum of fuss.

KITCHEN PLANNING AND EQUIPMENT

Being successful at keeping your last-minute preparations and cooking to a minimum may have a lot to do with how orderly and efficient your kitchen is and with the type of equipment you have. It goes without saying that kitchen equipment and utensils as well as electrical extras should be of good quality. Poorly designed or cheaply made items are never labour-saving.

THE KITCHEN

Nothing could be more annoying than having a meal almost ready to serve and then having to waste time searching for a fish slice or a bottle of dried herbs. A simple rearrangement of storage areas could be a big step towards maximum efficiency. Divide your cupboards and drawers to avoid having to search out packets or utensils. Racks are available which

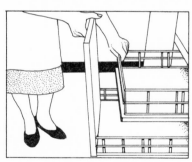

Racks on runners in drawers

are fixed or that pull out on telescopic runners. Make sure that everything you use regularly is in easy reach.

You should be able to move easily from sink to main work surface and then to the cooker. Moving a sink is expensive but it may be possible to add a new work surface near it — either by fitting a large cutting board over the

draining surface or by placing a table near the sink. A cover fitted over the sink or a hinged work top

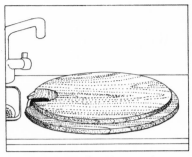

A cover over sink makes another surface

which is raised when needed are other ways to create extra work surface.

It may be a good idea to store regularly used condiments like mustard, vinegar, jam and sauces in a carousel on the table, thereby avoiding the need to get them out each meal time.

A kitchen with dining area opens up new possibilities for planning meals as it allows the cook to stay with the diners throughout the meal. Especially good for informal entertaining, this arrangement allows you to prepare omelettes, escalopes and other quickly made dishes without interrupting the flow of conversation. A serving hatch knocked through the dividing wall between kitchen and dining room is a good alternative. With these types of kitchen good ventilation is very important to keep heat, steam and cooking smells to a minimum. A fan-activated hood over the cooker is the most effective method.

THE COOKER

Most cookers come with automatic controls which enable you to set the oven to switch on at a pre-selected time and temperature. Food can be placed in the oven in the morning and be fully cooked when you come home in the evening. Most dishes can be placed in a cold oven and left without harm and brought up to the correct temperature. Make sure that anything put in the oven for cooking later is thoroughly chilled. For example, a casserole should not be at all warm from the initial preparation of frying the meat and vegetables, otherwise dangerous bacteria may develop.

By making minor adjustments it is possible to cook several different dishes at the same time and temperature. To slow down the cooking of a milk pudding or poached fruit, simply cover the dishes with kitchen foil or stand the dish in a hot water bath. Roast meat using the slow method along with braised vegetables and roast potatoes.

POTS AND PANS
Choose casseroles which can withstand freezing and which oven temperatures and which are attractive enough to use for serving and thus save on washing up. Make sure

Casserole dishes to suit all needs

they have tight-fitting lids which is important with slow cooking to prevent moisture from escaping.

GADGETS
Sharp knives (and a steel or sharpener) are essential in the kitchen, but the cook who wishes to keep preparation work to a minimum will also need some of the specialised gadgets available. Which you buy depends on your needs, though most cooks would include a potato peeler and vegetable brush. *Apple corers* and

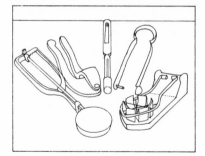

Specialised gadgets speed preparation

cherry stoners do their jobs very efficiently; *egg slicers* or *wedgers* are handy for making last-minute garnishes. A *garlic press* and *ice cream scoop* are extras you may also find worth acquiring. Wall can openers work faster and more easily than ordinary ones.

ELECTRICAL EQUIPMENT

It is all too easy to accumulate electrical appliances. Although they can help you to get through your work in the kitchen and are great time-savers, some may wind up gathering dust if you do not choose wisely. Most run off a 13-amp socket plug—if there are not enough in your kitchen to take all your appliances buy a panel of flying sockets.

The following items have features especially good for the busy cook who likes to prepare meals in advance.

FOOD PROCESSOR
With just the flick of a switch 450 g (1 lb) meat can be minced in 20 seconds. A food processor greatly cuts down on preparation work. It does most of the jobs of a mixer and blender, though it does not whisk egg whites well. It chops, minces, slices and grates as well as kneads bread. Many of the foods that you would normally need to prepare in advance can be done just before serving, therefore keeping them fresh. And if you do

a lot of batch cooking for the freezer, or cook large quantities at one time, then a food processor will be a great help with large chopping and slicing tasks.

SLOW COOKER
A slow cooker enables you to prepare soups, stews or casseroles and then leave them for up to 12 hours to cook. In this way you can prepare a dish in the morning and come home to a fully cooked meal—the slow cooker is ideal for making all-in-one meals. There is no risk of burning or boiling dry. Some models have a removable pot which can be used for serving and makes cleaning much easier.

MICROWAVE OVEN
Food can be cooked in a microwave in about one-third the time it takes to cook it conventionally. Many foods take even less time—a jacket potato will cook in 4 minutes, for example. A microwave oven is the perfect companion to food ready-prepared and frozen as thawing can be done in the microwave and reheating takes only a few minutes. Flavour, texture and colour remain unaltered when foods are reheated and there is little risk of burning or sticking to the dish.

There are a number of different models available with varying degrees of sophistication—which one you choose largely depends on what extent you intend to rely on the microwave for cooking. Cooking is done by microwave energy for a set time. It is necessary to be present during cooking to turn food or to stir it because all microwave ovens have 'hot spots' and do not cook food evenly. Turntables and stirrers help to reduce the amount of attention required. Cooking with a microwave oven is entirely different from conventional cooking. It is more precise and needs close attention for a short time. Some dishes may need to be finished off under the grill if a browned appearance or crisp texture is wanted.

The Clever Cook

In this chapter you will find tips on how to cope with everyday cooking, as well as more special occasions, including Christmas. When time permits, preserves can be made for year-round use, and when you are in a hurry, the freezer can be used as a reliable standby.

PLANNING AHEAD

Although preparing and cooking meals can be a real pleasure, if it is your responsibility day after day it can easily become a chore. But with a little foresight and imagination you can find ways to do it when the mood strikes, or when you have spare time and are not rushed. In other words, cook ahead, and ensure that feeding your family always remains an enjoyable task.

PLANNING MEALS
There's a lot to be said for writing down your weekly menu plans. It helps you to think of ways to keep within the family budget and to make best use of your time. You can plan to cook extra meat on one

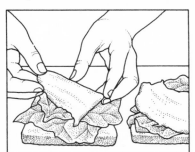

Serve leftover cold meat in sandwiches

night for serving later in the week or if you are having a family outing you could include pot-roasted meat for one meal and have leftover for serving cold in sandwiches. Plan different types of meal—not ones that all have to be started at the same time, or that all require last-minute attention.

Each meal should be nutrition-ally balanced and also include a variety of textures and colours as well as flavours. Avoid a sequence of rich sauces or too many pale-coloured dishes. You wouldn't want to serve a creamy soup followed by a fish pie with a syllabub for dessert. On the other hand a creamy soup is an excellent choice if the main course consists of grilled lamb chops and some brightly coloured vegetables. Make sure that the family are not begging for something crunchy to eat by the end of the meal. Offset a spicy meat dish with bland boiled rice or mashed potatoes.

SHOPPING
After noting what you have in store make out your shopping list. To save time always shop for several meals at a time. Most packaged foods are date stamped to tell you the minimum keeping time, after which flavour is impaired. Take advantage of fruit and vegetables when they are in season and low prices combine with best flavour.

Don't be too rigid about your list. An impulse buy may be a bargain, provided it doesn't mean having to juggle the entire meal plan. Also, you can't count on finding a certain ingredient, especially if it is fairly unusual. Have an alternative cut of meat or a different vegetable in mind in case what you originally planned turns out to be unavailable or exorbitantly priced.

COOKING A MEAL
To make life easier in the kitchen look at your chosen recipes and see how much can be made in advance. Does the recipe include a sauce (those without eggs or cream) which can be reheated without risk of curdling? Or you could make the stuffing before breakfast, or the dessert the night before.

Calculate the timing of each dish so that you can be sure you start cooking the one which takes longest first, and that all are ready together, or in the order required.

EASY ENTERTAINING

A successful dinner party starts with guests being greeted by a confident and calm host. Being organised is the key to success. Start by planning your menu well in advance and get as much as possible out of the way before guests arrive. Practical considerations like seating, table linen, flowers and fresh towels in the bathroom must be taken into account too. Buy your wine and any spirits well in advance, not forgetting garnishes like cocktail olives or onions.

A traditional three-course meal

For easy entertaining, stick to a traditional three-course meal. Any extras can consist of fruit and cheese *Never experiment*: always select dishes that you have made before. (To broaden your repertoire try out new dishes on your family first.)

Plan dishes which require only last-minute assembling, brief cooking or reheating. Start by choosing your main course, then pick a first and last course which balance it.

STARTERS
One certain way to make your entertaining easy is to avoid a hot first course altogether and serve something cold before guests assemble at the table. In this way you can easily slip off to the kitchen to do last-minute work on the main course. Crudités served

with a spicy mayonnaise are always popular; also good for serving informally are stuffed mushrooms, a pâté or a mousse with toast.

Soups are also good first courses as they can be prepared in advance and simply reheated if they are to be served hot. Add any milk, yogurt or cream when reheating to avoid curdling.

MAIN COURSES
Select a casserole or stew which can be made in advance and serve with vegetables which are cooked at the last minute. Conversely, serving grilled or fried foods, and have a vegetable casserole or ragout ready-prepared. If you plan to shallow-fry escalopes or steaks, then make sure you have enough frying pans to cope with all the frying at the same time. For

Equipment for deep-fat frying

deep-fat frying have everything ready beforehand, together with any last-minute garnishes.

DESSERTS
Most cold desserts can easily be made in advance. Gelatine-based desserts like cheesecakes and cold mousses only become firm after at least 4 hours in the refrigerator.

Serve light simple desserts after a substantial main course and rich luxurious ones after a light meal.

MEAT AND POULTRY

Meat and poultry, especially chicken, continue to be a favourite choice for many family meals. It's important for the busy cook to find a good friendly butcher and stick to him. If he appreciates your custom he will be more likely to do some of the more fiddly and time-consuming tasks such as boning a shoulder of lamb and chopping or mincing meat to the size you require for a particular dish.

Plan to buy enough meat to allow for leftovers which can be made into another main course. You may wish to buy enough meat at one time for the whole week and do most of your meat cooking at the weekend when you have time. Allow 100–150 g (4–5 oz) boneless meat per serving and 150–350 g (5–12 oz) meat on the bone per serving (depending on how much bone).

Bear in mind that the larger a piece of meat the longer it will keep: for example, minced meat should be used on the day of purchase, whereas a large joint will keep for up to 5 days in the coldest part of the refrigerator. If you do buy your meat all at once you may wish to cut it yourself, and for this you must have a good sharp kitchen knife. The food processor is a great time saver for chopping meat, but remember that chopped meat should not be

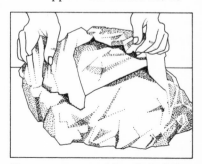

Keep meat wrapped loosely in foil

prepared more than 12 hours in advance or blood will ooze out and the meat become dry. Wrap meat loosely with foil to allow air to circulate, otherwise it will deteriorate rapidly. (Never leave meat in sealed plastic bags.)

Poultry should be used within 24 hours of purchase; frozen birds *must* be completely thawed before cooking. When preparing a bird for roasting, never place warm stuffing in a cold bird unless you are about to put it straight into a hot oven, otherwise dangerous bacteria may develop. Prepare stuffing in advance, but refrigerate it separately until just before roasting.

Although chops and steaks are always popular and take very little time to cook, they are expensive. To add variety to meals, choose from the more economical cuts and cook stews and casseroles.

STEWS, CASSEROLES AND BRAISES

Almost all stews and casseroles improve in flavour if made at least

Removing solid fat from stew

24 hours ahead. Allow them to cool, then cover and refrigerate. The fat will rise to the surface and become solid, making it easy to degrease the dish—especially important for oxtail and other fatty meats. They will keep covered in the refrigerator for up to 3 days.

Beef is the favourite meat for this long, slow and moist form of cooking, which tenderises the tougher cuts. Most cuts of pork and lamb are tender and so long

slow cooking is not so often used, but some cuts can make excellent casseroles. Boiling fowls are very good value, but tough and require slow cooking. When cooking stews and casseroles on the hob they must be very slowly simmered—if allowed to boil the meat will toughen. Stir occasionally to prevent sticking and check to see if more liquid is needed. Cooking these dishes in a casserole in the oven is easier, as no attention should be required provided that the temperature is sufficiently low, but unless other items can be cooked at the same time it is less economical. Single

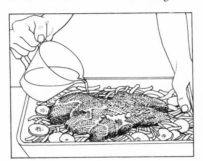

Moistening braised meat with stock

large pieces of beef are excellent braised in the oven on a bed of chopped vegetables moistened with stock.

If you plan to reheat a stew or casserole, undercook vegetables, particularly root vegetables which will crumble if overcooked, either by cutting in larger-than-usual pieces, or adding halfway through. Add green vegetables and any chopped fresh herbs when reheating. Enrich fricassees and blanquettes with egg and or cream when reheating to avoid curdling. Reheat in a 180°C (350°F) mark 4 oven. Sliced meats are best reheated with a little gravy added to keep them moist.

MARINADES

A marinade is a great way to prepare meats in advance. Flavoured with herbs and spices, a marinade will add flavour to meat and also help tenderise it.

Marinades also help prevent meat from spoiling and in some cases it may be left to marinate for several days. Immerse the meat in the

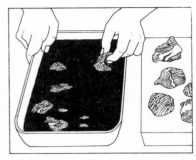

Immersing meat in a marinade

marinade, cover and refrigerate until ready for cooking. With poultry, flavour will penetrate better if it is skinned first.

FISH

Fish requires very little cooking time, making it a good choice for midweek family meals when you are on a tight schedule and have little time to spend in the kitchen. But it can be a fiddly task to prepare fish for cooking, so patronise a fishmonger who will clean and fillet fish for you. Otherwise, you can prepare fish up to 12 hours before cooking, but make sure you use a good sharp knife. Keep the fish in the refrigerator, loosely wrapped to prevent the flesh from drying out. The fish can then be grilled or fried. *Avoid overcooking*—most fish needs as little as 5 minutes on each side.

Allow 175–225 g (6–8 oz) of fish per serving, depending on whether it is a fillet or whole fish. Fresh fish should be cooked on the same day; smoked fish can be kept for 2–3 days in the refrigerator.

Fish needs to be kept moist as it easily dries out. Fish casseroles can be made in advance and reheated just before serving, but make sure that the fish is submerged in liquid. With white fish like cod and haddock, cook extra and use the leftovers for fish pies, fish cakes or croquettes, or to serve cold in a salad. To pre-cook fish for pies etc, cover with cold water and bring to the boil. Turn off the heat and leave for 5 minutes, then drain. With frozen fish, leave for 10–15 minutes. Do not be tempted to leave any longer as it will become soggy. The cooking liquid can be set aside as the basis for a sauce. Leave the fish to cool, then fork into flakes, removing the skin and bones.

Marinating is a good way to keep fish moist during storage.

Ceviche, a Mexican dish using raw fish, makes an excellent

Turning fish chunks in a marinade

dinner-party starter. Use firm white fish chunks and marinate in lemon juice for up to 12 hours, though 1 hour is all that is needed; turn the fish once during marinating. Salmon marinated in lime juice is also delicious. Toss the fish with chopped sweet peppers in a garlicky vinaigrette.

Once shellfish are removed from their shells they very quickly dry out. This is especially so with molluscs like mussels, oysters and scallops. Avoid preparing these in advance unless you wish to incorporate them in a cold fish salad or in a soup or sauce. Have ready pancakes or vol-au-vent cases to make a lunch dish which needs only last-minute assembling and reheating.

Remember that canned fish is a useful standby. Use canned tuna or salmon for mixing with rice or pasta for a quick midweek meal, or for making a party mousse.

COOK-AHEAD FISH DISHES

FISH CAKES

Makes 10

450 g (1 lb) old potatoes (peeled weight), cooked
350 g (12 oz) leftover cooked cod or haddock fillet, flaked
25 g (1 oz) butter or margarine
60 ml (4 tbsp) chopped fresh parsley
finely grated rind of $\frac{1}{2}$ lemon
salt and freshly ground pepper
plain flour
2 eggs, beaten
100 g (4 oz) fresh breadcrumbs
vegetable oil, for shallow frying

1 Mash the potatoes and stir in the fish, butter, parsley, lemon rind and seasoning to taste.

2 When the mixture is cool but not cold, turn out on to a lightly floured surface.

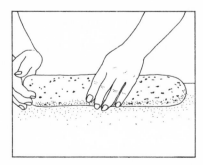

3 With floured hands, shape into a sausage about 38 cm (15 inches) long. Make sure that the surface is free from cracks.

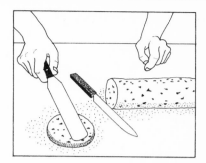

4 Cut the roll into ten 4 cm (1$\frac{1}{2}$ inch) slices. One at a time, place the slices on a floured surface and pat with a palette knife to level the surface and reduce the thickness to about 2 cm ($\frac{3}{4}$ inch).

5 Coat the fish cakes one at a time in the beaten eggs, then in the breadcrumbs. Chill in the refrigerator for at least 30 minutes or until required.

6 When ready to serve, put enough oil in a frying pan to come about halfway up the fish cakes. Heat until a cube of bread turns golden brown in 50–60 seconds. Lower in a few cakes and fry until golden brown. Turn over and cook for a further 5–10 minutes.

7 Drain well on absorbent kitchen paper while frying the remainder.

FREEZING INSTRUCTIONS
Prepare the fish cakes to the end of step 5. Open freeze on baking sheets until firm. Pack into rigid containers and return to freezer. Thaw for 2 hours only and complete as in steps 6 and 7.

FISH CROQUETTES

Makes 12

50 g (2 oz) butter or margarine

100 g (4 oz) plain flour

300 ml (½ pint) milk

350 g (12 oz) leftover, cooked white
fish, flaked

30 ml (2 tbsp) finely chopped
parsley

15 ml (1 tbsp) capers, roughly
chopped

5 ml (1 tsp) lemon juice

salt and freshly ground pepper

cayenne pepper

1 egg, beaten

50 g (2 oz) dried breadcrumbs

vegetable oil, for deep-frying

1 Melt the butter in a saucepan,
add half the flour and cook
over low heat, stirring with a
wooden spoon, for 2 minutes.

2 Remove the pan from the heat
and gradually blend in the
milk, stirring after each addition
to prevent lumps forming. Bring
to the boil slowly, then simmer for
2–3 minutes, stirring. Cover and
leave for at least 30 minutes until
cold.

3 Stir the fish into the sauce,
beating until smooth. Stir in
the parsley, capers and lemon
juice, mixing well. Season with
salt, pepper and cayenne.

4 Turn the mixture onto a
board, divide in half, then
into 12 fingers. With *lightly*
floured hands, roll each portion
into a sausage about 7.5 cm
(3 inches) long.

5 Coat the croquettes one at a
time in the beaten egg, then in
the breadcrumbs. Chill in the
refrigerator for at least 30 minutes
or until required.

6 When ready to serve, heat the
oil in a deep-frier to 180°C
(350°F). Place a few croquettes at
a time into a frying basket and
lower gently into the hot oil.
Deep-fry for 2–3 minutes or until
golden brown. Drain on absorbent
kitchen paper while deep-frying
the remainder.

FREEZING INSTRUCTIONS
Prepare the croquettes to the end
of step 5. Open freeze on baking

sheets until firm. Pack into a rigid
container and return to the
freezer. Thaw for 2 hours only;
complete as in step 6.

MARINADE FOR RAW FISH

Serves 4

5 ml (1 tsp) coriander seeds

1 dried red chilli, seeded and
roughly chopped

juice of 4 limes

juice of 2 lemons

30 ml (2 tbsp) olive oil

freshly ground black pepper

1 medium onion, skinned and
finely sliced

450 g (1 lb) fish fillets (monkfish,
plaice, sole), skinned

1 Crush the coriander seeds and
chilli to a fine powder in a
mortar. Mix with the lime juice,
lemon juice, olive oil, pepper and
onion rings. (Do not add salt as
this draws the juices out of the
fish making the dish very watery.)

2 Pour over the fish, mix well,
cover and chill in the
refrigerator for at least 6 hours or
until the fish turns opaque or
white.

FRUIT

A bowl of fruit saves many busy cooks from the time and trouble of making a dessert. The various textures, colours and flavours of fruit make it a good choice to finish off any meal, especially a substantial one where the refreshing taste of fruit is welcome.

Choose fruit which is slightly underripe for serving several days after buying. Store underripe fruit at room temperature; to speed up

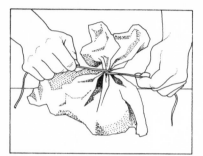

Ripen fruit in a brown paper bag

ripening, place the fruit in a brown paper bag and tie tightly. Store ripe fruit in the refrigerator. Pick over and wipe soft berry fruits, discarding any damaged ones. Other fruits can be washed in advance and given a good polish with absorbent kitchen paper. Grapes, however, should be washed just before serving to keep their bloom.

Gluts and other fruit bargains usually mean that the fruit is ripe and must be used very soon. Make sure that you have the time to prepare the fruit either for the freezer or for making preserves. Adding sugar to fruit will help keep it for longer in the refrigerator. Make fruit purées and freeze for 6–8 months, or store in the refrigerator for 2–3 days; use to make fools and fruit mousses or serve as a sauce for ice cream.

If you are after a trouble-free impressive dessert select exotic (though expensive) fruits such as mangoes, kiwi fruits and papayas

to add to a fruit salad. When serving cut-up fruit remember that bananas, apples and peaches should be left until the last moment and sprinkled with lemon juice to prevent discoloration. Lemon juice also heightens the flavour of a fruit salad. Keep cut fruit in the refrigerator, tightly wrapped with cling film.

Fruit puddings like crumbles and fruit pies can be made up to the baking stage in advance, or pre-baked, then warmed through just before serving. Meringue shells and pie cases can be made several days ahead of time and filled with fruit, cream or ice cream just before serving.

CHEESE

Whether you serve cheese on its own or with fruit, it makes an interesting and satisfying conclusion to a meal. Always keep cheeses well covered before serving, otherwise they will dry out around the edges very quickly. Wrap them individually to prevent flavours from mingling. They are best stored in an airtight container in the larder; if kept in the bottom of the refrigerator take out 30 minutes before serving. Soft cheeses will keep for up to 10 days and hard cheeses for up to 1 month.

Fresh cheeses like *fromage blanc* and *petits suisses* are ideal for serving with soft berry fruits. Cheddar and other English cheeses are good companions to apples and pears as well as nuts. Soft cheeses like Brie and Camembert go well with grapes.

VEGETABLES

Vegetables are a vital part of most meals because they add valuable nutrients and fibre and help to balance them. But it is important that they be prepared and cooked properly. It is all too easy to sacrifice vegetable texture, nutrition and flavour in the name of expediency.

Most vegetables can be prepared up to 12 hours before serving (but remember that there will be a nutrient loss); after that flavour is slightly impaired. They should be tightly covered with cling film and stored in the refrigerator until ready for cooking. Root vegetables such as potatoes and turnips should be kept in cold water in the coldest part of the refrigerator. (However, vitamin C, which is water soluble, starts to diminish.) Celeriac, Jerusalem artichokes and salsify need to be soaked in water with lemon juice or vinegar added to prevent discoloration.

Many vegetables need only to be cooked briefly before serving. Some, like carrots, green beans or cabbage, are best when they are still crisp and almost crunchy and in this way more nutrients are retained. They can be slightly undercooked, then rinsed under

Rinsing vegetables to arrest cooking

cold running water to retain colour and arrest further cooking. Reheat quickly in butter just before serving.

Vegetable dishes can be cooked in a number of different

ways to help keep last-minute preparations to a minimum.

Braised Vegetables like red cabbage, celery, chicory and celeriac are delicious when braised, that is, slowly cooked in very little liquid until they become soft. Leave until cold, cover and refrigerate, then reheat slowly.

Stewed Ratatouille (vegetable ragout) is the classic example of a dish which improves greatly if made well ahead of serving (see recipe on page 22). Stewed vegetable dishes will keep for 2–3 days in the refrigerator. They are also good served cold (allow them to come to room temperature for best flavour).

Stuffed Serve vegetables as an accompaniment stuffed with breadcrumbs, or as a main course stuffed with rice and chopped meat. The stuffing can be made in advance and the case filled up to 12 hours ahead. Bake in the oven to finish. Choose from tomatoes, aubergines, mushrooms and onions.

Puréed Most vegetables can be puréed, either as a convenient way of storing them in the freezer for later use in soups, or as a vegetable dish accompaniment. Boiled or steamed vegetables can be quickly puréed in a blender or food processor or put through a sieve or vegetable mill. Leave until cold, cover and refrigerate. To reheat, season, add a dash of cream and heat slowly, stirring often. Root vegetables can be put in the oven.

COOK-AHEAD VEGETABLE DISHES

LAYERED FRENCH-STYLE POTATOES

Serves 4–6

900 g (2 lb) potatoes, peeled
30 ml (2 tbsp) Dijon mustard
30 ml (2 tbsp) snipped chives
300 ml ($\frac{1}{2}$ pint) milk or chicken stock
salt and freshly ground pepper
25 g (1 oz) butter, melted

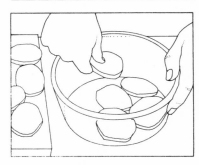

1 Cut the potatoes into 1 cm ($\frac{1}{2}$ inch) slices and arrange one layer in a greased 1.1 litre (2 pint) ovenproof dish.

2 Combine the mustard, chives, liquid and seasoning. Pour some over the potato layer. Repeat layers of potato and mustard/chive dressing, finishing with potato.

3 Brush the top layer of potato with butter, and sprinkle with salt and pepper. Cover the dish with foil and leave in a cool place until required.

4 When ready to serve, bake in the oven at 180°C (350°F) mark 4 for $1\frac{3}{4}$–2 hours until the potatoes are tender when pierced with a fork.

STUFFED PEPPERS

Serves 4

40 g ($1\frac{1}{2}$ oz) butter
1 onion, skinned and chopped
100 g (4 oz) streaky bacon, rinded and chopped
4 tomatoes, skinned and sliced
100 g (4 oz) long grain rice, cooked
60 ml (4 tbsp) grated Cheddar cheese
salt and freshly ground pepper
4 large green peppers
50 g (2 oz) fresh breadcrumbs
150 ml ($\frac{1}{4}$ pint) chicken stock

1 Melt 25 g (1 oz) of the butter in a heavy-based saucepan, add the onion and bacon and fry gently until golden brown. Add the tomatoes, cooked rice, half of the cheese and seasoning to taste.

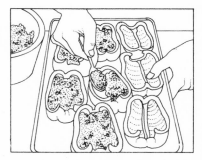

2 Halve the green peppers lengthways; remove pith and seeds. Place them in a single layer in a greased ovenproof dish and spoon in the stuffing.

3 Mix the remaining cheese with the breadcrumbs and sprinkle over the stuffing. Pour the stock around the peppers and top each with a knob of butter. Leave in a cold place until required.

4 When ready to serve, bake in the oven at 190°C (375°F) mark 5 for 15–20 minutes, or until the peppers are tender.

RICE AND PASTA

Rice and pasta are essential store-cupboard items to add variety to meals. They can be served in place of potatoes as an accompaniment to meat or poultry, or as a main course in their own right. They are both an excellent way to stretch leftover meat and vegetables.

RICE

Rice takes very well to a number of seasonings and flavourings so that family members need never tire of it. Cook extra rice to use cold in a rice salad or as part of a stuffing for vegetables or meat. Allow 50 g (2 oz) raw rice per serving.

Fluffing up rice before serving

Plain boiled rice can be made up to 24 hours ahead of serving. To reheat, dot with butter or margarine and place in a 180°C (350°F) mark 4 oven for 20 minutes. Fluff up with a fork and serve. Risottos, paellas and pilaffs can be reheated in the same way.

PASTA

Along with dried pasta, a good supply of fresh pasta, now so readily available, is a good reserve in the freezer. It takes only 1–2 minutes to cook from frozen and with a good pasta sauce on hand you can quickly serve a delicious no-fuss dinner party dish. Cook extra pasta shapes to add to soups and salads (pasta to be served cold

should not be tossed in butter which hardens it).

Many pasta sauces can be made in advance and gently reheated. Delicious dishes can also be made in minutes by tossing pasta in such basics as cheese, eggs and cream and topping with grated Parmesan cheese. Fresh herbs, canned fish or crisp bacon are good last-minute additions.

Cooked pasta is best stored coated in a sauce, and in made-up dishes such as macaroni cheese and lasagne (which also freeze well). It will keep for several days in the refrigerator and can be reheated in a 180°C (350°F) mark 4 oven for 20 minutes or so until bubbling.

COOK-AHEAD SAUCES TO SERVE WITH PASTA

MILANESE SAUCE

Serves 4

25 g (1 oz) butter
½ onion, skinned and chopped
50 g (2 oz) mushrooms, chopped
225 g (8 oz) tomatoes, skinned and chopped, or 425 g (15 oz) can tomatoes, drained
5 ml (1 tsp) sugar
1 bay leaf
few sprigs of thyme
pinch of grated nutmeg
salt and freshly ground pepper
50 g (2 oz) ham, chopped
50 g (2 oz) tongue, chopped

1 Melt the butter in a heavy-based saucepan, add the onion and mushrooms and fry gently for 3–5 minutes until soft. Stir in the tomatoes, sugar, herbs, nutmeg and seasoning to taste. Cover and simmer gently for about 20 minutes, until the sauce has thickened and developed a good flavour.

2 Add the ham and tongue and simmer, uncovered, for a further 5–10 minutes. Cool, then chill in the refrigerator or freeze until required. Reheat for 5–10 minutes until bubbling, then taste and adjust seasoning before serving.

BOLOGNESE SAUCE

Serves 4

knob of butter
50 g (2 oz) streaky bacon, rinded and chopped
1 small onion, skinned and chopped
1 carrot, peeled and chopped
1 celery stick, washed, trimmed and chopped
225 g (8 oz) lean minced beef
100 g (4 oz) chicken livers, chopped
15 ml (1 level tbsp) tomato purée
150 ml (¼ pint) dry white wine
300 ml (½ pint) beef stock
salt and freshly ground pepper

1 Melt the butter in a large saucepan, add the bacon and fry for 2–3 minutes. Add the onion, carrot and celery and fry for a further 5 minutes until just browned.

2 Add the beef and brown lightly, then stir in the chicken livers and cook for a further 3 minutes. Add the tomato purée and wine and simmer for a few minutes more.

3 Stir in the stock and seasoning to taste and simmer for 30–40 minutes, until the meat is tender. Cool, then chill in the refrigerator or freeze until required. Reheat for 5–10 minutes until bubbling, then taste and adjust seasoning before serving.

PORTABLE FOOD

Whether it's for a simple packed lunch or an elegant picnic, food must be the kind that can be prepared ahead of serving, and it must travel well. Food must remain fresh and appetising during storage, which may not always be in ideal conditions. Sandwiches are always a good choice, but there are many other possibilities for adding variety to portable foods.

Choose foods that are firm but moist, and that will not become limp in transport. Filled things like sausage rolls, Scotch eggs and meat pasties which can be eaten with the fingers are good, as are cold cooked chicken portions, and omelettes, cooked, cooled and sliced. Hard-boiled eggs, pizzas and quiches also add interest to picnics.

Remember too that a can of sardines or tuna fish, a jar of olives and some homemade pickles are good storecupboard items for last-minute outings. Buy good fresh bread and some cheeses and you have satisfying picnic fare.

A carefully planned picnic does not have everything made ahead. Some dishes are best assembled at the site and in fact make picnics more enjoyable. Include plenty of fresh salad ingredients and fresh fruits, plus several sharp knives and a small cutting board for slicing. Take along a good home-made vinaigrette. Cold vegetables like marinated mushrooms and ratatouille can be made in advance and travel well.

Plastic drinking mugs and paper plates make picnics easy. If you regularly enjoy picnics it may be worth having a hamper. It not only adds style to a picnic but it saves searching for bottle and can openers and assembling plates and

cups as everything is ready for transport. Vacuum flasks, especially ones with wide-neck openings, open up possibilities of taking along hot foods such as soups or a warming chilli con carne or beef stew.

If you take a flask of tea or coffee, carry the milk separately in a special plastic container, or an unopened carton; it ruins the taste if added in advance.

DEVILLED CHICKEN DRUMSTICKS

Makes 6

| 150 ml (¼ pint) vegetable oil |
| 5 ml (1 tsp) mild curry powder |
| 5 ml (1 tsp) paprika |
| 2.5 ml (½ tsp) ground allspice |
| 2.5 ml (½ tsp) ground ginger |
| 6 chicken drumsticks |

1 Make the marinade. Whisk together the oil and spices.

2 Skin the chicken drumsticks. Using a sharp knife, make 3 shallow slashes in the flesh of each one.

3 Spoon the marinade over the chicken, cover and chill in the refrigerator for 4–5 hours, turning occasionally.

4 Place the chicken drumsticks in a roasting tin just large enough to hold them in a single layer. Pour over the marinade.

5 Bake in the oven at 200°C (400°F) mark 6 for 40–45 minutes, basting frequently and turning once. Cool on a wire rack.

6 When completely cool, wrap a little foil over the end of each drumstick, or top with a cutlet frill. Pack together in a rigid container for transporting.

SANDWICHES

A good sandwich starts with good bread; don't overlook wholewheat, rye or pumpernickel breads which can go a long way in adding variety to sandwiches. Fresh bread is hard to slice thinly enough for sandwiches, so use a day-old loaf, or buy it ready sliced.

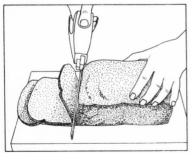

Using an electric carving knife

Alternatively, use an electric carving knife, which will happily cut newly baked bread into wafer-thin slices. Removing the crusts

should not be necessary—fresh air creates good appetites. Pitta bread makes a good pocket for filling with a variety of salads and cold meats. Warm the bread in the oven and wrap tightly in foil. Do not grill the bread or it will become brittle when cold.

Make sure butter for spreading is at room temperature; or use tub margarine. Both provide a good waterproof protection for the bread, preventing it from becoming soggy, and stick the sandwich together. Spread it right to the edges.

Choose fillings with contrasting textures and cover the bread completely—there is no skimping with a good sandwich. Tuck in lettuce and tomatoes at the last-minute to prevent sogginess. Mayonnaise is a good addition.

Sandwiches can be made in advance and stored overnight. Wrap them individually in cling film and store in the refrigerator.

BEEF PATTIES
Makes 10

1 medium onion, skinned and chopped

450 g (1 lb) lean minced beef

1 beef stock cube, crumbled

15 ml (1 tbsp) chopped fresh oregano or 5 ml (1 tsp) dried

1 egg, beaten

salt and freshly ground pepper

45 ml (3 tbsp) vegetable oil

225 g (8 oz) plain flour

2.5 ml (½ tsp) salt

75 g (3 oz) lard

50 g (2 oz) butter or margarine

beaten egg, to glaze

1 Mix together the onion, minced beef, crumbled stock cube, oregano and egg. Season lightly.

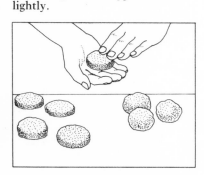

2 With wet hands, shape the mixture into 10 flattened balls.

3 Heat the oil in a large frying pan and cook the patties for 4–6 minutes on each side. Drain and cool on absorbent kitchen paper.

4 Put the flour and salt in a bowl, add the lard and butter or margarine and rub in with the fingertips. Mix to a soft dough with about 40 ml (8 tsp) cold water.

5 Turn the dough on to a floured surface and knead lightly until smooth. Roll out thinly, then stamp out 10 rounds with a 6.5 cm (2½ inch) fluted cutter and 10 rounds with a 10 cm (4 inch) fluted cutter.

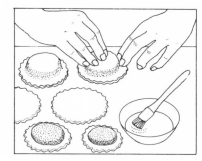

6 Place the cool patties on the smaller circles of dough, brush the edges with beaten egg and cover with the larger circles. Seal the edges well.

7 Cut the pastry trimmings into tiny rounds. Brush the patties with beaten egg, decorate with the rounds and brush with more beaten egg.

8 Place the patties on a baking sheet and bake in the oven at 190°C (375°F) mark 5 for 20–25 minutes until golden. Cool on a wire rack for 30 minutes before packing in a rigid container.

CARROT AND PINEAPPLE SLAW
Serves 4

20 ml (4 tsp) vegetable oil

20 ml (4 tsp) vinegar

20 ml (4 tsp) pineapple juice from can

pinch of sugar

dash of mild curry paste

4 rings canned pineapple

450 g (1 lb) carrots, scraped

60 g (4 tbsp) sultanas

salt and freshly ground pepper

1 Put the oil in a rigid container with the vinegar, pineapple juice, sugar and curry paste. Cover and shake well to mix.

2 Using scissors, snip the pine-pineapple into the dressing. Grate in the carrot, using the coarse side of the grater. Stir in the sultanas and seasoning to taste.

3 Seal the container and chill in the refrigerator until required.

SPINACH AND APPLE SALAD
Serves 8

450 g (1 lb) fresh spinach

60 ml (4 tbsp) orange juice

30 ml (2 tbsp) vegetable oil

15 ml (1 tbsp) wine vinegar

salt and freshly ground pepper

2 large eating apples

1 Pull off any thick stalks from the spinach. Wash the spinach, drain well and shred. Chill in a large plastic container.

2 Mix the orange juice, oil, vinegar and seasoning together. Quarter, core and slice the apples and stir into the dressing. Pour into a lidded container, cover and chill.

3 Toss the spinach and dressing together just before serving.

CHRISTMAS COUNTDOWN

To ensure that you have a festive but calm Christmas, start shopping and planning for your holiday entertaining well in advance. There's no substitute for a complete holiday checklist covering Christmas lunch and all the traditional Christmas goodies plus table decorations. It may seem daunting at first, but with foresight and organisation Christmas time can be the pleasure it is supposed to be.

The best way to plan a Christmas period of eating without frustration in the kitchen is to keep meals, other than Christmas lunch, flexible. A roast gammon or ham along with leftover turkey will provide several meals if you plan a good selection of winter salads to serve with them. Have some cold desserts such as a fruit compote or brandied peaches on hand or make a Christmas cheesecake with a cranberry topping, or a chestnut pavlova—meringue layers can be made several days before assembling and stored in an airtight container.

A freezer will be of enormous help when preparing for Christmas. All baking can be done about 3 months in advance. Freeze pies and breads uncooked and bake them nearer the time of serving . . . part of the enjoyment of Christmas is the delicious smells wafting from the kitchen. Make your own mincemeat; providing brandy is added it can be made at the beginning of December or even earlier. Christmas puddings are traditionally made at the end of November.

- Buy a bird large enough to serve on Boxing Day. Calculate the size of bird you need on the basis of 350–450 g (12 oz–1 lb) for small birds, 350 g (12 oz) for medium birds, 225 g (8 oz) for large birds per serving. Order it as early as the end of November.

- Make sure you allow shelf space in the freezer for Christmas food. Mark packages for Christmas.

- If you make your own preserves and pickles, pot some in small attractive jars and set aside for entertaining over Christmas; they also make excellent last-minute gifts.

- Make your sauces in advance and have a few on hand to enliven leftovers. Keep all sauces in the refrigerator.

Sauce	In advance
Brandy Butter	2 weeks
Cumberland Sauce	1 week
Cranberry Sauce	1 week
Bread Sauce	2 days
Horseradish Sauce	1 day (using fresh cream)
Vinaigrette	1 week

- Make a large quantity of white sauce and store in 300 ml ($\frac{1}{2}$ pint) portions. It will keep for up to 5 days in the refrigerator. Add cheese or herbs to it when reheating and serve with vegetables or use as the basis for a turkey casserole.

- Peel potatoes up to 24 hours in advance. Soak in cold water and keep in the coldest part of the refrigerator.

- Peel chestnuts and cook the day before serving. Leave to cool and store tightly wrapped in the refrigerator along with ready-trimmed Brussels sprouts.

- Check drinks cupboard and take advantage of Christmas specials offered by off-licences. *Buy or order early*. There are usually special offers for buying wine by the case. Remember to stock up on ice cubes. Turn them into polythene bags; to keep cubes separate spray them with soda water.

RICH CHRISTMAS PUDDING

Makes 1 pudding to serve 8

100 g (4 oz) prunes
175 g (6 oz) currants
175 g (6 oz) seedless raisins
175 g (6 oz) sultanas
100 g (4 oz) plain flour
1.25 ml ($\frac{1}{4}$ tsp) grated nutmeg
1.25 ml ($\frac{1}{4}$ tsp) ground cinnamon
2.5 ml ($\frac{1}{2}$ tsp) salt
75 g (3 oz) fresh breadcrumbs
100 g (4 oz) shredded suet
100 g (4 oz) soft dark brown sugar
25 g (1 oz) blanched almonds, chopped
finely grated rind of $\frac{1}{2}$ lemon
150 ml ($\frac{1}{4}$ pint) brown ale
2 eggs, beaten

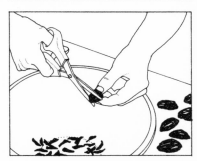

1 Snip the prunes into small pieces into a large bowl, discarding the stones.

2 Half-fill a steamer or large saucepan with water and put it on to boil. Grease a 1.4 litre (2$\frac{1}{2}$ pint) pudding basin.

3 Add the remaining ingredients to the prunes and stir well until evenly mixed.

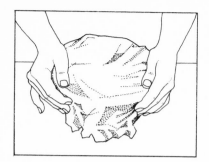

4 Spoon the mixture into the prepared basin, pushing down well. Cover with greased, pleated greaseproof paper and foil. Steam for about 8 hours.

5 Remove the foil covering, but leave the greaseproof paper in position. Allow to cool, then cover with a clean dry cloth or foil and store in a cool place for at least 2 weeks before serving.

6 To reheat, steam for 2½ hours. Turn out on to a warmed serving plate and serve with brandy or rum butter.

MINCEMEAT

Makes about 2.5 kg (5½ lb)

450 g (1 lb) currants

450 g (1 lb) sultanas

450 g (1 lb) seedless raisins

225 g (8 oz) chopped mixed peel

225 g (8 oz) hard cooking apples, peeled, cored and grated

100 g (4 oz) blanched almonds, chopped

450 g (1 lb) dark soft brown sugar

175 g (6 oz) shredded suet

5 ml (1 tsp) grated nutmeg

5 ml (1 tsp) ground cinnamon

finely grated rind and juice of 1 lemon

finely grated rind and juice of 1 orange

300 ml (½ pint) brandy

1 Place the dried fruits, peel, apples and almonds in a large bowl. Add all the remaining ingredients and mix thoroughly.

2 Cover the mincemeat and leave to stand for 2 days. Stir well and put into jars. Cover. Leave for at least 2 weeks to mature before using.

FESTIVE CHRISTMAS CAKE

20.5 cm (8 inch) round rich fruit cake

apricot glaze (see page 144)

550 g (1¼ lb) bought marzipan

900 g (2 lb) royal icing (see page 144)

ribbon and Christmas cake decorations such as Santa Claus, snowmen, robins, reindeer or Christmas trees, to finish

1 At least 14–20 days before required, place the cake on a 23 cm (9 inch) cake board. Brush with apricot glaze and cover with marzipan (see page 144). Loosely cover the cake and store in a cool dry place for 4–5 days.

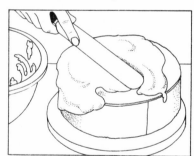

2 Using half the royal icing, roughly spread the icing over the top and side of the cake. Leave to dry for 24 hours. Keep the remaining icing in a covered container.

3 Spoon the remaining icing on top and roughly smooth it over with a palette knife.

4 Using a palette knife or the back of a teaspoon, pull the icing into well-formed peaks.

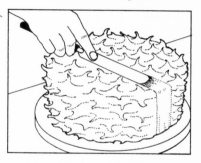

5 Using a palette knife, smooth a path down the centre of the top and side of the cake. Leave to dry for about 24 hours.

6 Place a piece of ribbon along the pathway, securing the ends with pins. Arrange the decorations on top, securing them if necessary with little dabs of freshly made icing. Leave to dry for at least another 24 hours, ideally about 1 week before Christmas.

7 Once iced, the cake will keep fresh without an airtight tin, but when dry, protect it by covering with a cake dome or box.

TO COVER A CAKE WITH MARZIPAN

Cover the cake with marzipan 1 week or—at the latest—2 days before applying the first coat of royal icing. If the marzipan is not given enough time to dry out, oil from the paste may discolour the icing.

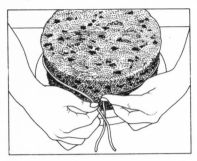

1 To cover a round or square cake, first measure round the cake with a piece of string.

2 Dust your work surface liberally with icing sugar and roll out two thirds of the marzipan to a rectangle, half the length of the string and twice the depth of the cake.

3 Trim the edges of the marzipan neatly with a knife, then cut the rectangle in half lengthways.

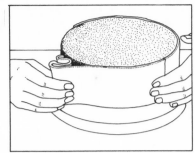

4 Place the cake upside down on a board and brush the sides with apricot glaze. Gently lift the marzipan and place it firmly in position round the cake. Smooth joins with a palette knife and roll a jam jar lightly round the cake.

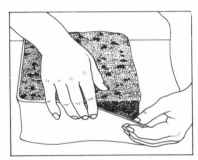

5 For a square cake, position one strip of marzipan on one side of the cake and fold it round to cover a second side. Repeat for the other two sides. Keep the top edge of the cake square with the marzipan.

6 Smooth the joins with a palette knife and mould any surplus marzipan into the bottom edge.

7 Brush the top of the cake with apricot glaze. Dust your working surface with icing sugar and roll out the remaining marzipan to a round or square the same size as the top of the cake.

8 Lift the marzipan on to the top of the cake with the rolling pin. Lightly roll with the rolling pin, then smooth the join and leave to dry for at least 2 days.

APRICOT GLAZE

Makes 150 ml (¼ pint)

100 g (4 oz) apricot jam
30 ml (2 tbsp) water

Put the jam and water in a saucepan and heat gently, stirring, until the jam softens. Bring to the boil and simmer for 1 minute. Sieve the glaze and use while still warm.

ROYAL ICING

Makes about 900g (2 lb)

4 egg whites
900 g (2 lb) icing sugar
15 ml (1 tbsp) lemon juice
10 ml (2 tsp) glycerine

1 Whisk the egg whites in a bowl until slightly frothy. Then sift and stir in about a quarter of the icing sugar with a wooden spoon. Continue adding more sugar gradually, beating well after each addition, until about three quarters of the sugar has been added.

2 Beat in the lemon juice and continue beating for about 10 minutes until the icing is smooth.

3 Beat in the remaining sugar until the required consistency is achieved, depending on how the icing will be used.

4 Finally, stir in the glycerine to prevent the icing hardening. Cover and keep for 24 hours to allow air bubbles to rise to the surface.

PRESERVES

Putting food by is an age-old tradition which ensures that seasonal fruits and vegetables do not get wasted and are available all year round. Making jams, jellies and marmalade, or spicy pickles, relishes and chutneys is still one of a cook's most rewarding tasks, as they should be not only less expensive but better than anything in the shops.

Special equipment is not essential for making preserves, but some help to make the job easier. Preserving pans are thick-based with slanting sides which help prevent overboiling of a hot mixture. Choose a good one made from heavy aluminium or stainless steel; it can double as a pan for making pickles and chutneys which contain a lot of vinegar. Brass, copper and iron react with vinegar causing a metallic flavour, so pans made of these metals must not be used when making pickles and chutneys. A nylon sieve should be used as metal can discolour fruit and it also reacts adversely with vinegar. A long-handled wooden spoon makes stirring easier and if you make jellies then a jelly bag is worth having. Other useful aids for regular jam-makers are a sugar thermometer and a jam funnel.

Jars must be in perfect condition with no cracks or chips. Collect old coffee, jam and pickle jars; you can also buy jars for jams, special preserving jars and Kilner jars. Sterilising jars before use is essential—make sure they are thoroughly clean by washing in hot soapy water and rinsing well. Dry off the jars in a cool oven, at 140°C (275°F) mark 1, and use while warm so that they do not crack when filled with boiling jam or chutney.

Equipment needed for making preserves

JAMS, JELLIES AND MARMALADE

Which preserve you make is largely a matter of family preference, but there are several points that the busy cook needs to consider. When a favourite fruit is abundant, it may not be a convenient time for you to make preserves. If you have a freezer, then most fruits can be frozen for use later (Seville oranges, for example, have a short season in January and February), otherwise only buy a large amount if you know you will have the time to preserve them then and there.

Jams, jellies and marmalade all require two stages of cooking, first to soften the fruit and extract its pectin, and then to boil it with sugar until setting point is reached. The first stage of cooking can take as little as 10 minutes with soft fruits, but citrus fruits, which are used for marmalades, may need as much as 4 hours to soften their tough skins. After the first cooking, jellies must be strained; this usually requires at least 6 hours, so you must allow for two blocks of time when making them.

FRUIT

There must be sufficient quantities of pectin, acid and sugar present in fruit for preserves to get their characteristic firm set. Getting the balance right is what successful preserve making is all about, so it is important to follow recipes exactly until you get the knack of creating your own combinations of fruits. Fruit which is just ripe or only slightly underripe should be used; pectin content diminishes in overripe fruit. Fruits low in acid or pectin can still be used, but they require the addition of a fruit high in pectin and/or acid. Lemon juice helps to bring out the flavour of the fruit but commercially bottled pectin may be used according to manufacturer's instructions. Allow 30 ml (2 tbsp) lemon juice for every 2 kg (4 lb) fruit. When acid is all that's required, citric or tartaric acid is just as good. Allow 2.5 ml ($\frac{1}{2}$ tsp) for every 2 kg (4 lb) fruit with poor setting quality.

SUGAR

Once the fruit has softened sugar is added; sugar not only affects setting quality, it also acts as a preservative. If too little sugar is used then the preserve may not set and can become mouldy during storage. Too much sugar and the preserve may crystallise and become sticky. To ensure that the preserve sets well, the sugar must be added after the fruit has sufficiently softened—which is why uncooked fruit for preserving should not be frozen in a sugar pack.

First dissolve the sugar slowly in the hot fruit, then boil briskly until setting point is reached. To help retain the natural colour and flavour of the fruit, it is important that you do not greatly exceed the stated time for boiling in the recipe testing.

TESTING FOR A SET

A sugar thermometer can be placed in, or stood in or attached to, the

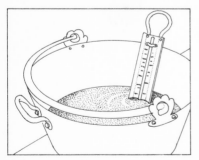

Using a sugar thermometer

side of the pan. When the temperature reaches 104°C (220°F), a set should be obtained. Or use the saucer test: place a little spoonful of the preserve on a chilled saucer, leave to cool, then push your finger gently through it. If the surface wrinkles, setting point has been reached. The pan should be removed from the heat during this

Using finger to test for a set

test. If setting point has not been reached, then return to the boil for a few more minutes and test again. Once setting point has been reached, remove any scum from the surface with a skimmer or slotted spoon before potting.

JELLIES

To make a clear, firmly set jelly, the fruit is strained and the sugar is added to the extracted juice. Fruit is cooked to a pulp and left to drip through a jelly bag

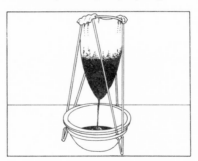

Straining fruit pulp through jelly bag

(though you can improvise by using a double thickness of fine cloth, the four corners tied to an upturned chair) until all the juice is strained off. Fruit high in pectin can be re-cooked after the first straining in a little water and then strained again. Measure the juice and for every 600 ml (1 pint) juice, add 45 g (1 lb) sugar to fruit juices high in pectin and 375 g (12 oz) sugar for juice with a medium pectin content. The fruit juice and sugar are then boiled until setting point is reached.

MARMALADE

To prepare citrus fruits, the juice is squeezed out and the peel is cut thinly or thickly according to how you like your marmalade. The pips and membranes, which are rich in pectin, are loosely tied in a piece of muslin and cooked along with the citrus juice, peel and water. A large amount of water is used with marmalade because of the long cooking, during which it should reduce by about half. After

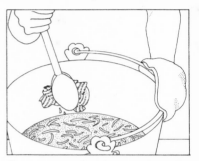

Squeezing musling bag to extract liquid

cooking, squeeze the muslin bag with a wooden spoon to extract as much liquid as possible. An alternative method is to cook the fruit whole: after simmering the fruit is cut and the pips and membranes boiled for a few minutes before adding the sugar.

When cooking frozen oranges, use the whole-fruit cooking method and add one-eighth extra weight of fruit to offset pectin loss during freezing.

POTTING, COVERING AND STORING

Jars holding around 450 g (1 lb) or 1 kg (2 lb) are the usual choices. If they do not have screw tops you can buy jam pot covering sets which consist of waxed discs, Cellophane covers and elastic bands. The jars should be warm and placed on a heat-resistant surface such as a chopping board or a pile of newspapers to prevent cracking when ladling in the hot preserve. Fill the jars up to the bottom of the neck. Some whole-fruit jams and marmalades should cool for about 15 minutes before potting, otherwise the fruit will rise. Cover the surface of the pre-

Covering preserve with waxed disc

serve with a waxed disc, waxed side down; this is to exclude air. Then immediately cover with a lid or a dampened Cellophane round secured with a rubber band. Label with contents and date.

Store in a cool, dry, dark place for up to 1 year. If stored for longer, the flavour and colour will start to deteriorate although the preserve is perfectly safe to eat. Sometimes mould growth occurs on the top of a jam; in this case the jam is not safe to eat.

PICKLES, CHUTNEYS AND RELISHES

All of these are a good way to add interest to any meal, be it hot or cold, elaborate or plain.

Many kinds of fruit and vegetables are used, ranging from onions, red cabbage, cucumbers, cauliflower, apples and dried fruit to aubergines, bananas and pears.

Pickles are preserved either raw or lightly cooked. They should look attractive, so produce must be perfect. For most types no more than washing and trimming is needed. Chutneys and relishes need more preparation as ingredients must be finely chopped. Chutneys are cooked long and

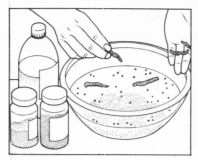

Spices add extra flavour to vinegar

slowly to produce a jam-like consistency. Relishes are cooked briefly or not at all.

All are preserved in vinegar, which must have an acetic acid content of at least 5%. Distilled (white) vinegar is best for light-coloured pickles; malt is traditional for pickled onions and perfectly good for chutneys. The more expensive wine and cider vinegars give the best flavour.

Spices add the finishing touch. They are usually ground for chutneys and relishes, left whole for pickles.

MAKING PICKLES

Before vinegar is added, many vegetables and some fruits are first salted to remove excess water which would dilute the strength of the vinegar during storage, and therefore diminish the keeping qualities. Vegetables with a high

Layer with salt before adding vinegar

water content like marrows, tomatoes and cucumbers are layered with salt. Use 15 ml (1 tbsp) salt for every 450 g (1 lb)

vegetables. Other vegetables like cauliflower and onions are covered with a brine solution of 50 g (2 oz) salt dissolved in 600 ml (1 pint) water for every 45 g (1 lb) vegetables. The vegetables are left, covered, for up to 24 hours, then drained and rinsed. Fruits do not require brining as they are usually lightly cooked to evaporate the surplus moisture before pickling.

Pouring vinegar on pickles

Pack vegetables loosely and attractively in warmed jars. Pour over cold vinegar for crisp pickles and hot vinegar for softer ones. Fill jars as full as possible, making sure that the vinegar covers the contents. Cover immediately with airtight vinegar-proof lids such as preserving skin, plastic or plastic-lined screw tops or large corks which have been first boiled. (The acid will eat into plain metal lids.)

For sweet fruit pickles, sugar is added to the vinegar, the liquid is reduced to concentrate the flavour and poured over the fruit.

Leave pickles to mature for 3 months before serving. Most will keep for up to 1 year, but red cabbage pickles should be served within 2–3 weeks.

MAKING CHUTNEYS AND RELISHES

These are much the simplest preserves to make. All the ingredients, including sugar which gives the sweet-sour flavour, are simmered until there are no pools of liquid left on the surface. For chutneys this can take as long as 4 hours. Only occasional stirring is needed. Pot and store as pickles.

USING THE PRESSURE COOKER

Use the pressure cooker to save time when making preserves. It is especially good for making marmalade and softening hard fruits for jellies. Not only is there a great time saving but the fruit retains its flavour and colour beautifully. Always consult manufacturer's instructions before using your pressure cooker for preserving. Although the entire preserve can be made in the pressure cooker pan, only the preliminary cooking and softening of the fruit can be done actually under pressure. After adding the sugar and any lemon juice the preserve must be boiled in the open pan for about 15 minutes. Never fill the pan more than half full; use half the amount of water given in a standard recipe. Add half of this when the fruit is cooked under pressure. The second half is added with the sugar. Cook citrus fruits for 20 minutes at medium (10 lb) pressure. Release pressure at room temperature.

FRUITS IN ALCOHOL

For a delicious storecupboard dessert that you can boast is homemade, fruits in alcohol are well worth making. They are made by preserving lightly poached fruits like peaches, apricots and plums in equal parts of sugar and alcohol. Brandy is usually used, but more unusual mixtures contain kirsch or orange-flavoured liqueurs. The sugar syrup can be flavoured with whole spices like cinnamon and cloves, and for an attractive appearance the spices can be added to the jar. Fruits in alcohol should be potted and covered in the same way as jams.

BUSY COOK'S GUIDE TO JAMS, JELLIES AND MARMALADE

● Cook frozen fruit from frozen to prevent discoloration.

● Chop citrus fruit peel in the chopper attachment of a food mixer or in a food processor. Do not use a coarse mincer as it produces a paste-like marmalade.

● Soak citrus peel overnight to help soften it.

● For jams made with stone fruits, the stones will float to the surface after cooking and can be removed with a slotted spoon. Cherries are an exception, however, and their stones should be removed beforehand, with a cherry stoner.

● Grease the bottom of the preserving pan with butter to help prevent sticking during cooking.

● Use granulated sugar which is the most economical; or more expensive preserving and lump sugars which give a clearer set and cause less scum. Brown and caster sugars produce a lot of scum.

● Warm the sugar in a 140° (275°F) gas mark 1 oven before adding it to the fruit and it will dissolve more quickly when stirred into the fruit.

● Warm the jars in the oven at the same time as the sugar. Rest them on their sides on the grooves of the oven racks.

● Have saucers chilling in the refrigerator ready for testing.

● Adding a knob of butter after the sugar has dissolved helps reduce foaming.

● Scald a jelly bag so the fruit juice runs clean through and is not absorbed by the fabric.

● Don't rush the straining by squeezing the bag—this results in a cloudy mixture.

● Wipe filled jars clean with a cloth that has been wrung out in hot water while they are still warm.

● Save jars during the year so that you don't have to hunt at the last minute for the odd jar. Those holding 450 g or 900 g (1 lb or 2 lb) are the most useful sizes as you can buy covers for these sizes.

PECTIN CONTENT OF FRUITS AND VEGETABLES USED IN PRESERVING

Good	Medium	Poor
Cooking apples	Dessert apples	Bananas
Crab-apples	Apricots	Carrots
Cranberries	Bilberries	Cherries
Currants	Blackberries	Elderberries
(red and black)	Cranberries	Figs
Damsons	Greengages	Grapes
Gooseberries	Loganberries	Marrows
Lemons	Mulberries	Medlars
Limes	Plums	Melons
Seville oranges	Raspberries	Nectarines
Plums (some varieties)		Peaches
Quinces		Pineapple
		Rhubarb
		Strawberries

PRESERVE RECIPES

GOOSEBERRY JELLY

Makes about 1.8 kg (4 lb)

2 kg (4½ lb) gooseberries, washed

water

sugar

1 Put the gooseberries in a pre-serving pan with water to cover. Bring to the boil, then simmer gently for ¾–1 hour until the fruit is soft and pulpy. Stir from time to time.

2 Spoon the fruit pulp into a jelly bag or cloth attached to the legs of an upturned stool and leave to strain into a large bowl for at least 12 hours.

3 Discard the pulp remaining in the jelly bag. Measure the extract and return it to the pan with 450 g (1 lb) sugar for each 600 ml (1 pint) extract. Heat gently, stirring, until the sugar has dissolved, then boil rapidly for about 15 minutes.

4 Test for a set, then remove any scum with a slotted spoon. Pot and cover.

───── VARIATIONS ─────

GOOSEBERRY MINT JELLY
Cook the gooseberries with a few sprigs of mint and add finely chopped mint to the jelly before potting.

GOOSEBERRY AND ELDERFLOWER JELLY
Tie two large elderflower heads in a piece of muslin. When the jelly has reached setting point, remove from the heat, add the muslin bag and stir around in the hot jelly for about 3 minutes. This will produce a good flavour that is not over-dominant.

STRAWBERRY JAM

Makes about 2.3 kg (5 lb)

1.6 kg (3½ lb) strawberries, washed and hulled

45 ml (3 tbsp) lemon juice

1.4 kg (3 lb) sugar

knob of butter

1 Put the strawberries in a pre-serving pan with the lemon juice. Simmer gently, stirring occasionally, for 20–30 minutes until really soft.

2 Take the pan off the heat, add the sugar and stir until dis-solved. Add a knob of butter and boil rapidly for about 20 minutes.

3 Test for a set, then remove any scum with a slotted spoon.

4 Allow the jam to cool for 15–20 minutes, stir gently, pot and cover.

DRIED APRICOT JAM

Makes about 2.3 kg (5 lb)

450 g (1 lb) dried apricots, soaked in 1.7 litres (3 pints) water overnight

juice of 1 lemon

1.4 kg (3 lb) sugar

50 g (2 oz) blanched almonds, split

knob of butter

1 Put the apricots in a pre-serving pan with the soaking water and lemon juice. Simmer for about 30 minutes until soft, stir-ring from time to time.

2 Remove the pan from the heat and add the sugar and almonds. Stir until the sugar has dissolved, then add a knob of butter and boil rapidly for 20–25 minutes, stirring frequently to prevent sticking.

3 Test for a set, then remove any scum with a slotted spoon. Pot and cover.

SEVILLE ORANGE MARMALADE

Makes about 4.5 kg (10 lb)

1.4 kg (3 lb) Seville oranges, washed

juice of 2 lemons

3.4 litres (6 pints) water

3 kg (6 lb) sugar

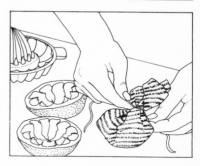

1 Halve the oranges and squeeze out the juice and pips. Tie the pips, and any membrane that has come away during squeezing, in a piece of muslin.

2 Slice the orange peel thinly or thickly, as preferred, and put it in a preserving pan with the fruit juices, water and muslin bag. Simmer gently for about 2 hours until the peel is really soft and the liquid reduced by about half.

3 Remove the muslin bag, squeezing it well and allowing the juice to run back into the pan. Add the sugar, stirring until it has dissolved, then boil the mixture rapidly for about 15–20 minutes. Test for a set, then remove any scum with a slotted spoon.

4 Allow the marmalade to cool for 15–20 minutes, stir gently, pot and cover.

LEMON CURD

Makes about 700 g (1½ lb)

finely grated rind and juice of 4
    medium lemons

4 eggs

100 g (4 oz) butter

350 g (12 oz) caster sugar

1 Place all the ingredients in the
    top of a double saucepan or in
a bowl standing over a pan of
simmering water. Stir until the
sugar has dissolved and continue
heating gently for about 20
minutes until the curd thickens.

2 Strain into jars and cover.
    Store for about 1 month only.

——————— VARIATION ———————

The fresh lemon juice can be
replaced with 180 ml (12 tbsp)
artificial lemon juice. To give
extra tang, add the grated rind of 1
fresh lemon.

SWEETCORN RELISH

Makes about 2.5 kg (5½ lb)

6 corn cobs, trimmed, with leaves
    and silk removed

½ a small white cabbage, trimmed
    and roughly chopped

2 medium onions, skinned and
    halved

1½ red peppers, seeded and
    quartered

10 ml (2 tsp) salt

30 ml (2 tbsp) plain flour

2.5 ml (½ tsp) turmeric

175 g (6 oz) granulated sugar

10 ml (2 tsp) mustard powder

600 ml (1 pint) distilled (white)
    vinegar

1 Cook the corn cobs in boiling
    water for 3 minutes, then
drain. Using a sharp knife, cut the
corn from the cobs.

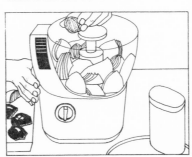

2 Coarsely mince the cabbage,
    onions and red peppers and
combine with the corn.

3 Blend the salt, flour, turmeric,
    sugar and mustard together in
a saucepan, then gradually stir in
the vinegar. Heat gently, stirring,
until the sugar has dissolved, then
bring to the boil. Add the
vegetables and simmer for 25–30
minutes, stirring occasionally. Pot
and cover.

BEETROOT AND HORSERADISH RELISH

Makes about 1.4 kg (3 lb)

50 g (2 oz) fresh horseradish

450 g (1 lb) raw beetroot

1 medium onion, skinned

225 g (8 oz) cooking apples

450 ml (¾ pint) malt vinegar

225 g (8 oz) granulated sugar

1 Peel and grate the horseradish.
    Peel the beetroot, then shred
or grate coarsely. Chop the onion.
Peel, quarter, core and roughly
chop the apples.

2 Place all the ingredients in a
    medium-sized saucepan and
heat gently until the sugar
dissolves.

3 Boil gently, uncovered, for
    about 1¼ hours until the
ingredients are tender and the
contents well reduced. Pot and
cover.

PICKLED RED CABBAGE

about 1.4 kg (3 lb) firm red
   cabbage, finely shredded

2 large onions, skinned and sliced

60 ml (4 tbsp) salt

2.3 litres (4 pints) spiced vinegar
   (see below)

15 ml (1 tbsp) soft light brown
   sugar

1 Layer the cabbage and onion
in a large bowl, sprinkling each
layer with salt, then cover and
leave overnight.

2 Next day drain the cabbage
and onion thoroughly, rinse
off the surplus salt and drain
again. Pack into jars.

3 Pour the vinegar into a pan
and heat gently. Add the sugar
and stir until dissolved. Leave to
cool, then pour over the cabbage
and onion and cover immediately.
Use within 2–3 weeks as the
cabbage tends to lose its crispness.

SPICED VINEGAR

Makes 1.2 litres (2 pints)

1 litre (2 pints) vinegar

30 ml (2 tbsp) blade mace

15 ml (1 tbsp) whole allspice

15 ml (1 tbsp) whole cloves

18 cm (7 inches) cinnamon stick

6 peppercorns

1 small bay leaf

1 Place the vinegar, spices and
bay leaf in a saucepan, bring to
the boil and pour into a bowl or
bottles. Cover to preserve the
flavour and leave to marinate for 2
hours.

2 Strain through muslin, pour
into clean bottles and seal with
airtight and vinegar-proof tops.
An even better result is obtained if
the spices are left to stand in
unheated vinegar for 1–2 months.

DRIED FRUIT PICKLE

Makes about 1.4 kg (3 lb)

450 g (1 lb) granulated sugar

300 ml (½ pint) distilled (white)
   vinegar

10 ml (2 tsp) whole cloves

10 ml (2 tsp) whole allspice

1 cinnamon stick

pared rind of 1 small lemon

2.5 ml (½ tsp) ground ginger

900 g (2 lb) dried mixed fruit,
   soaked in cold water overnight

1 Put the sugar and vinegar in a
preserving pan and heat gently
until the sugar dissolves.

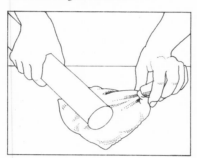

2 Place the cloves, allspice,
cinnamon stick and lemon rind
in a muslin bag. Crush lightly.

3 Add the bag to the vinegar and
sugar. Stir in the ground
ginger and bring to the boil. Cook
for 5–7 minutes until reduced and
syrupy, with about 700 ml (1¼
pints) remaining.

4 Put the dried fruit in a
separate pan with the soaking
water. Cover and simmer until
tender. Drain, then pack into
warm jars. Cover completely with
the hot reduced vinegar. Seal in
the usual way.

5 Keep for several weeks before
eating. Store in the
refrigerator after opening.

PICKLED ONIONS

Makes about 2 kg (4 lb)

2 kg (4 lb) pickling onions

450 g (1 lb) salt

4.5 litres (8 pints) water

1.2 litres (2 pints) spiced vinegar
   (see below left)

1 Place the onions, without skinning, in a large bowl. Dissolve
half the salt in half the water, pour
the brine over the onions and leave
for 12 hours.

2 Skin the onions, then cover
with fresh brine, made with
the remaining salt and water.
Leave for a further 24–36 hours.

3 Drain and rinse the onions
well and pack them into jars.
Pour the spiced vinegar over the
onions and cover the jars
immediately with airtight and
vinegar-proof tops. Leave for 3
months before use.

TOMATO AND SWEET RED PEPPER CHUTNEY

Makes about 1.5 kg (3 lb)

900 g (2 lb) ripe tomatoes

225 g (8 oz) onions

1 red chilli

1 sweet red pepper

300 ml (½ pint) distilled (white)
   vinegar

125 g (4 oz) demerara sugar

5 ml (1 tsp) salt

5 ml (1 tsp) paprika

1.25 ml (¼ tsp) chilli powder

1 Skin and roughly chop the
tomatoes and onions. Seed and
finely chop the chilli and pepper.

2 Place all the ingredients in a
medium saucepan and heat
gently until the sugar dissolves.

3 Boil gently, uncovered, for
about 1½ hours until the
vegetables are tender and the
chutney of a thick pulpy consistency, stirring occasionally. Pot
and cover.

COOK-AHEAD AND THE FREEZER

A freezer is a great aid to cooking ahead if kept well stocked with pre-cooked dishes, meat packs, vegetables and other ingredients including pastry and bread doughs.

Good freezer candidates are stews, casseroles, soups, stocks, sauces, cooked meats, fruit pies, bread and cakes: anything that takes too long to prepare when dinnertime is only 30 minutes away, freezes well and can then be served up quickly after thawing. But be careful to choose things your family will always eat: a good practice is to cook double or triple amounts of favourite dishes, serve one and freeze the rest.

A few points to remember when cooking for the freezer: with stews, add watery vegetables like courgettes when reheating; also potatoes, rice and pasta in case of overcooking. Frozen fat can spoil flavour, so degrease after chilling.

Add single cream, soured cream and yogurt on reheating, as they separate during freezing, create extra volume and waste space. Freeze soups as purées and add stock, milk or cream to thin down before serving. Season dishes on reheating as freezing affects the flavour of spices and seasonings.

When cooking in bulk be sure you have done all necessary shopping and that there is space for open freezing and storing what you make. Don't overload the freezer as food must freeze quickly to prevent large ice crystals forming. They damage food and alter flavour, texture and even colour. Too much food at a time slows freezing down. Follow the maker's instructions on using the fast freeze switch. As a general rule freeze no more than a tenth of your freezer's capacity. This means that you should freeze no more than 5 kg (11 lb) of food in a 50 kg (110 lb) freezer (about 170 litres or 6 cubic feet).

PACKING

Pack food in practical serving portions. You may want a few larger dinner-party packs, and if your family has an irregular time schedule, then a few single portions may be in order — especially useful if you heat food in a microwave. Remember that several packs can be reheated, but one large portion may only produce unwanted leftovers. Smaller portions also thaw and heat more quickly than large ones. Use shallow containers for food for the same reason — the deeper the container filled with food the longer it will take to thaw and heat.

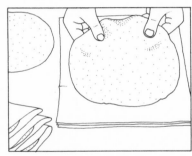

Interleaving pancakes with paper

Single items of food like fish fillets or pancakes should be packed with paper interleaved between them and then wrapped so that you can remove only those required at one time. Consider also whether it suits your family to freeze cakes and cooked fruit pies in serving portions rather than

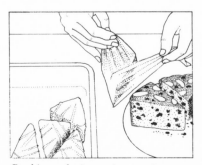

Packing cake in serving portions

whole, and pack them accordingly.

Using preformers is an excellent way to freeze liquid dishes. They are especially good for freezing soups and casseroles, freeing the container for another use, and they also take up a minimum of freezer space. Line a casserole or other

Lining casserole dish with foil

rigid container with foil and pour or spoon in the food to be frozen. Once frozen, the contents can be removed, overwrapped, and returned to the freezer. When it is time to serve the dish it can be neatly inserted into the original dish and reheated.

When freezing stews, casseroles or fruits in syrup, solid pieces should be completely submerged in the liquid with no protruding pieces otherwise they may get freezer burn. As with all liquid dishes, always leave 1 cm ($\frac{1}{2}$ inch) headspace to allow for expansion during freezing. With other foods all air must be excluded from the packages. Heat sealing is a secure way to seal polythene bags and they make convenient boil-in-the-bags.

Along with the date and contents, labels should give information about finishing the dish such as adding seasonings, thickening or any liquid.

THAWING AND REHEATING

Most cooked dishes can be reheated from frozen and this helps to preserve flavour, texture and colour. Cooking from frozen is essential for vegetables, but other cooked dishes can be thawed before reheating. This is more of an economy measure than anything else, for example, to reheat a stew from frozen, needs 1 hour in a 200°C (400°F) mark 6 oven then a further 40 minutes at 180°C (350°F) mark 4. A thawed stew will only need 20–40 minutes at 180°C (350°F) mark 4. Reheating can also be done on the hob. If frozen, break up chunks with a fork to speed up reheating. Do not re-freeze thawed raw food unless it is cooked first, cooled quickly, then frozen.

FREEZER STANDBYS

Have these on hand to save time on last-minute preparations. This is a great way to use up leftovers.

STOCKS AND SAUCES

Make your own 'stock cubes' by

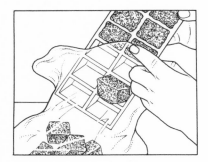

Storing frozen stock cubes

freezing stock in ice-cube trays until solid, then storing them in polythene bags (a well-reduced stock will be concentrated in flavour). Use as a convenient way to flavour soups and stews. Cubes of leftover sauces are also handy for flavouring.

CHEESE

Pack grated cheese in a polythene bag; the cheese will stay separate so you can shake out only as much as needed.

CHOCOLATE

When you feel like indulging in a little chocolate cookery, make chocolate squares, curls or leaves; freeze in rigid containers, interleaving layers to prevent crushing.

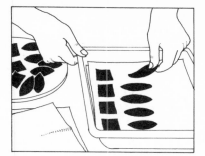

Interleaving chocolate shapes

Use for decoration while still very cold, but allow 10 minutes to thaw.

WHIPPED CREAM

Freeze leftover cream by piping in rosettes on to baking parchment

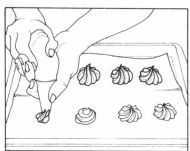

Piping rosettes on to baking parchment

on a tray. Open freeze until solid, then pack in rigid containers, interleaving layers to prevent crushing. Use from frozen to decorate, but allow 10 minutes to thaw.

JUICE OR RIND OF ORANGES AND LEMONS

When using just the rind or the juice of citrus fruits in a recipe, freeze the unused parts in a small container. For convenience in later recipes, make sure you state the quantity for each portion frozen. Grate rind before freezing.

BREADCRUMBS

Make fresh breadcrumbs and pack in polythene bags—the crumbs will stay separate. Thaw for 30 minutes if using to coat for frying, otherwise use from frozen. Buttered crumbs can also be frozen ready for use as toppings to be browned under the grill. Open

freeze, then pack in polythene bags in useable quantities.

CROÛTONS

Open freeze on trays until solid, then pack in a polythene bag. Reheat from frozen for 5–10 minutes in the oven at 200°C (400°F) gas mark 6.

HERBS

Freeze whole sprigs of herbs then, to avoid chopping them, crumble while still frozen into soups and stews; herbs will be too wet to use

Crumbling frozen herbs into soup

as a garnish. Alternatively, freeze chopped herbs with water in ice-cube trays (as for stock above), then transfer to a polythene bag.

Use straight from the freezer as an addition to stews, casseroles and sauces.

BUTTER BALLS

These take time to make when needed, but a few stored in the freezer—even those left over from a party—are handy for almost instant use.

PARSLEY BUTTER

This is ideal for topping steaks, chops and other grills such as fish. Cream 250 g (8 oz) unsalted butter until smooth. Beat in the grated rind and juice of 1 lemon, 60 ml (4 tbsp) chopped fresh parsley, and salt and pepper. Form into a long sausage shape between sheets of waxed or non-stick paper. Re-firm in the fridge or freezer and cut into 50 g (2 oz) portions. Wrap each in foil. Alternatively, freeze the butter roll whole and cut off slices as required. Make a neat parcel, seal and label. Use straight from the freezer.

Basic Recipes

These recipes for stocks, sauces and dressings can all be made in advance. The pancakes, pastries and crumble topping can even be frozen for later use.

STOCKS, SAUCES AND DRESSINGS

CHICKEN STOCK

Makes 1.1–1.4 litres (2–2½ pints)

carcass and bones of a cooked chicken

1.4–1.7 litres (2½–3 pints) cold water

1 onion, skinned and sliced

1 carrot, peeled and sliced

1 celery stick, washed, trimmed and sliced

bouquet garni (optional)

1 Break down the carcass and bones of the cooked chicken, and make sure to include any skin and chicken scraps.

2 Put in a pan with the water, onion, carrot, celery and the bouquet garni, if using.

3 Bring to the boil, skim with a slotted spoon, then cover and simmer for 3 hours.

4 Strain the stock thoroughly, discarding the bones and vegetables, then leave to cool. When cold, remove all traces of fat.

BEEF STOCK

Makes about 1.4 litres (2½ pints)

450 g (1 lb) shin of beef, cut into pieces

450 g (1 lb) marrow bone or knuckle of veal, chopped

1.7 litres (3 pints) cold water

bouquet garni

1 onion, skinned and sliced

1 carrot, peeled and sliced

1 celery stick, washed, trimmed and sliced

1 To give a good flavour and colour, brown the bones and meat in the oven (exact temperature is not important) before using.

2 Put in a pan with the water, bouquet garni and vegetables. Bring to the boil, skim with a slotted spoon, then cover and simmer for 5–6 hours.

3 Strain the stock thoroughly, discarding the bones, meat and vegetables, then leave to cool. When cold, remove all traces of fat.

BASIC WHITE (POURING) SAUCE

Makes 300 ml (½ pint)

15 g (½ oz) butter

15 g (½ oz) plain flour

300 ml (½ pint) milk

salt and freshly ground pepper

1 Melt the butter in a saucepan. Add the flour and cook over low heat, stirring with a wooden spoon, for 2 minutes. Do not allow the mixture (roux) to brown.

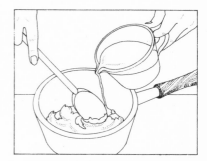

2 Remove the pan from the heat and gradually blend in the milk, stirring after each addition to prevent lumps forming. Bring to the boil slowly and continue to cook, stirring all the time, until the sauce comes to the boil and thickens.

3 Once thickened, simmer the sauce very gently for a further 2–3 minutes. Season with salt and freshly ground pepper.

COATING SAUCE

Follow recipe for Pouring Sauce (see left), but increase butter and flour to 25 g (1 oz) each.

CHEESE SAUCE

Follow the recipe for the Pouring Sauce or Coating Sauce (see above). Before seasoning, stir in 50 g (2 oz) grated **Cheddar cheese** and 2.5 ml ($\frac{1}{2}$ tsp) **mustard**.

MAYONNAISE

Makes about 350 ml (12 fl oz)

3 egg yolks

7.5 ml (1$\frac{1}{2}$ tsp) dry mustard

7.5 ml (1$\frac{1}{2}$ tsp) salt

2.5 ml ($\frac{1}{2}$ tsp) freshly ground pepper

7.5 ml (1$\frac{1}{2}$ tsp) sugar (optional)

450 ml ($\frac{3}{4}$ pint) sunflower oil or $\frac{1}{2}$ olive oil and $\frac{1}{2}$ vegetable oil

45 ml (3 tbsp) white wine vinegar or lemon juice

1 Put the egg yolks in a bowl with the seasonings and sugar and beat with a whisk. Continue beating and add 150 ml ($\frac{1}{4}$ pint) of the oil about a drop at a time.

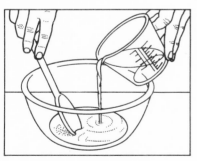

2 Once the mixture starts to thicken, continue adding the oil in a thin stream. Add the vinegar or lemon juice, beating constantly.

3 Add the remaining oil 15 ml (1 tbsp) at a time or in a thin stream, beating continually until it is completely absorbed.

TOMATO MAYONNAISE

Prepare as above, but add **2 tomatoes**, skinned, seeded and diced; **3 small spring onions**, trimmed and chopped; **3.75 ml ($\frac{3}{4}$ tsp) salt** and **15 ml (1 tbsp) vinegar**.

GARLIC MAYONNAISE

Skin **2 medium-sized garlic cloves** and crush with some of the salt; add to the mayonnaise.

CUCUMBER MAYONNAISE

Prepare as above but add **90 ml (6 tbsp) finely chopped cucumber** and 7.5 ml (1$\frac{1}{2}$ tsp) salt.

FRENCH DRESSING

Makes about 300 ml ($\frac{1}{2}$ pint)

75 ml (5 tbsp) red or white wine vinegar*

10 ml (2 tsp) Dijon or made English mustard

10 ml (2 tsp) salt

5 ml (1 tsp) freshly ground pepper

10 ml (2 tsp) sugar (optional)

2 garlic cloves, crushed (optional)

200 ml ($\frac{1}{3}$ pint) oil*

1 For a creamy dressing blend the ingredients in an electric blender or food processor.

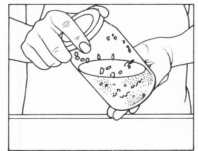

2 For a thinner dressing, shake vigorously in a screw-topped jar.

* Try also **tarragon vinegar** in dressings for tomatoes or potatoes; **thyme vinegar** with eggs or mushrooms; **cider vinegar** with fruits. **Lemon juice** can be substituted for vinegar as well.

* **Sunflower oil** alone or half and half with **olive oil** is pleasant. **Walnut oil** also adds interest.

PANCAKES, PASTRIES AND TOPPINGS

CRUMBLE TOPPING

Serves 4–6

175 g (6 oz) plain flour

75 g (3 oz) margarine or butter

50 g (2 oz) sugar

Put the flour in a bowl, then rub in the fat with the fingertips until the mixture is the texture of fine crumbs. Stir in the sugar.

This mixture may be kept in the refrigerator for 3–4 days; it can also be frozen—pack in a polythene bag and freeze for up to 3 months.

Add 5 ml (1 tsp) **ground cinnamon, mixed spice** or **ginger** to the flour before rubbing in the fat.

Add 50 g (2 oz) chopped **crystallised ginger** to the crumb mixture before using.

Add the finely **grated rind of 1 orange or lemon** to the crumb mixture before using.

Roughly crush 30 ml (2 tbsp) **cornflakes** and add them to the rubbed-in mixture with **demerara sugar** in place of granulated sugar.

PANCAKES

Makes 8 pancakes

125 g (4 oz) plain flour

pinch of salt

1 egg

300 ml ($\frac{1}{2}$ pint) milk

lard or vegetable oil

1 Mix the flour and salt to- gether in a bowl. Make a well in the centre and break in the egg. Add half the liquid, then gradually work in the flour from the sides of the bowl. Beat until smooth.

2 Add the remaining liquid gradually. Beat until the in- gredients are well mixed.

3 Heat a little lard or oil in a small frying pan, running it around the pan to coat the sides. Pour in a little batter, tilting the pan to form an even coating.

4 Place over moderate heat and cook until golden underneath, then turn with a palette knife and cook the other side. Slide the pancake on to a plate lined with greaseproof paper. Repeat.

SHORTCRUST PASTRY

175 g (6 oz) plain flour

pinch of salt

75 g (3 oz) butter or block margarine and lard

about 30 ml (2 tbsp) cold water

1 Mix the flour and salt together in a bowl. Cut the fat into small pieces and add it to the flour.

2 Using both hands, rub the fat into the flour between finger and thumb tips until the mixture resembles fine breadcrumbs.

3 Add the water, sprinkling it evenly over the surface. Stir it in with a round-bladed knife until the mixture begins to stick to- gether in large lumps.

4 With one hand, collect the mixture together and knead lightly for a few seconds to give a firm, smooth dough. The pastry can be used straight away, but is better allowed to 'rest' for about 30 minutes. It can also be wrapped in cling film and kept in the refrigerator for a day or two.

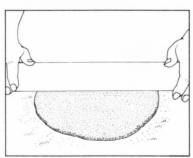

5 *To roll out:* sprinkle a very little flour on a working surface and the rolling pin, not on the pastry, and roll out the dough evenly in one direction only, turn- ing it occasionally. The ideal thickness is usually about 0.3 cm ($\frac{1}{8}$ inch). Do not pull or stretch the pastry. When cooking short- crust pastry, the usual oven tem- perature is 200–220°C (400– 425°F) mark 6–7.

FLAN PASTRY

100 g (4 oz) plain flour

pinch of salt

75 g (3 oz) butter or block margarine and lard

5 ml (1 tsp) caster sugar

1 egg, beaten

1 Mix the flour and salt together in a bowl. Cut the fat into small pieces, add it to the flour and rub it in as for shortcrust pastry until the mixture resembles fine breadcrumbs. Stir in the sugar until evenly mixed.

2 Add the egg, stirring with a round-bladed knife until the ingredients begin to stick together in large lumps.

3 With one hand, collect the mixture together and knead lightly for a few seconds to give a firm, smooth dough.

4 Rest and roll out as for short- crust pastry and use as required. When cooking flan pastry the usual oven temperature is 200°C (400°F) mark 6.

ROUGH PUFF PASTRY

225 g (8 oz) plain flour

pinch of salt

75 g (3 oz) butter or block margarine

75 g (3 oz) lard

about 150 ml ($\frac{1}{4}$ pint) cold water

squeeze of lemon juice

beaten egg, to glaze

1 Mix the flour and salt together in a bowl. Cut the fat (which should be quite firm) into cubes about 2 cm ($\frac{3}{4}$ inch) across.

2 Stir the fat into the flour without breaking up the pieces. Add enough water and lemon juice to mix to a fairly stiff dough.

3 Turn the dough on to a lightly floured surface, then roll out into an oblong three times as long as it is wide. Fold the bottom third up and the top third down.

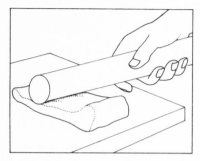

4 Turn the pastry so that the folded edges are at the sides. Seal the ends of the pastry by pressing lightly with a rolling pin.

5 Repeat this rolling and folding process three more times, turning the dough so that the folded edge is on the left hand side each time.

6 Wrap the pastry loosely in greaseproof paper and leave it to rest in the refrigerator or a cool place for about 30 minutes before using.

7 Roll out the pastry on a lightly floured surface to 0.3 cm ($\frac{1}{8}$ inch) thick and use as required. Brush with beaten egg before baking. The usual oven temperature for rough puff pastry is 220°C (425°F) gas mark 7.

PUFF PASTRY

450 g (1 lb) strong plain flour
pinch of salt
450 g (1 lb) butter
about 300 ml ($\frac{1}{2}$ pint) cold water
15 ml (1 tbsp) lemon juice
beaten egg, to glaze

1 Mix the strong plain flour and pinch of salt together in a large bowl.

2 Cut 50 g (2 oz) off the butter and pat the remainder with a rolling pin into a slab 2 cm ($\frac{3}{4}$ inch) thick.

3 Rub the 50 g (2 oz) butter into the flour with the finger and thumb tips. Stir in enough water and lemon juice to make a soft, elastic dough.

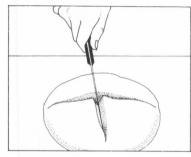

4 Turn the dough on to a lightly floured surface, then knead until smooth. Shape into a round and cut through half the depth in a cross shape.

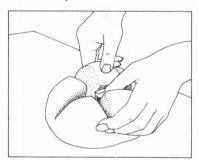

5 Open out the flaps to form a star. Roll out, keeping the centre four times as thick as the flaps.

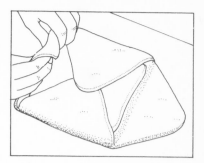

6 Place the slab of butter in the centre of the dough and fold over the flaps, envelope-style. Press gently with the rolling pin.

7 Roll out into a rectangle measuring about 40 × 20 cm (16 × 8 inches). Fold the bottom third up and the top third down, keeping the edges straight. Seal the edges by pressing with the rolling pin.

8 Wrap the pastry loosely in greaseproof paper and leave it to rest in the refrigerator or a cool place for about 30 minutes.

9 Put the pastry on a lightly floured surface with the folded edges to the sides and repeat the rolling, folding and resting sequence five times.

10 After the final resting, roll out the pastry on a lightly floured surface and shape as required. Brush with beaten egg before baking. The usual oven temperature for puff pastry is 230°C (450°F) mark 8.

FLAKY PASTRY

225 g (8 oz) plain flour

pinch of salt

75 g (3 oz) butter or block
  margarine

75 g (3 oz) lard

about 150 ml ($\frac{1}{4}$ pint) cold water

squeeze of lemon juice

beaten egg, to glaze

1 Mix the flour and salt
together in a bowl. Soften the
fat by working it with a knife on a
plate, then divide it into four equal
portions.

2 Add one quarter of the fat to
the flour and rub it in between
finger and thumb tips until the
mixture resembles fine
breadcrumbs.

3 Add enough water and lemon
juice to make a soft elastic
dough, stirring it in with a round-
bladed knife.

4 Turn the dough on to a lightly
floured surface and roll out
into an oblong three times as long
as it is wide.

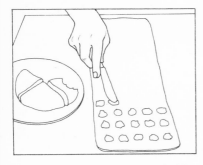

5 Using the round-bladed knife,
dot another quarter of the fat
over the top two-thirds of the
pastry in flakes, so that it looks
like buttons on a card.

6 Fold the bottom third of the
pastry up and the top third
down, and turn it so that the
folded edges are at the side. Seal
the edges of the pastry by pressing
with a rolling pin.

7 Re-roll as before and repeat
the process twice more until
the remaining portions of fat have
been used up.

8 Wrap the pastry loosely in
greaseproof paper and leave it
to rest in the refrigerator or a cool
place for at least 30 minutes before
using.

9 Roll out the pastry on a
lightly floured surface to
0.3 cm ($\frac{1}{8}$ inch) thick and use as
required. Brush with beaten egg
before baking. The usual oven
temperature for flaky pastry is
220°C (425°F) gas mark 7.

PÂTE SUCRÉE

100 g (4 oz) plain flour

pinch of salt

50 g (2 oz) caster sugar

50 g (2 oz) butter, at room
  temperature

2 egg yolks

1 Sift the flour and salt together
on to a cool surface, ideally a
marble slab.

2 Make a well in the centre of
the mixture and add the sugar,
butter and egg yolks.

3 Using the fingertips of one
hand, pinch and work the
sugar, butter and egg yolks
together until well blended.
Gradually work in all the flour,
adding a little water if necessary to
bind it together.

4 Turn the dough on to a lightly
floured surface and knead
lightly until smooth. Wrap loosely
in foil or cling film and leave it to
rest in the refrigerator or a cool
place for about 1 hour.

5 Roll out the pastry on a lightly
floured surface and use as
required. The usual oven temperature for pâte sucrée is 190°C
(375°F) mark 5.

BAKING BLIND

Baking blind is the process of
baking a pastry case without the
filling—essential if the filling is
to be uncooked or if it only requires a short cooking time. First
shape the pastry into the baking
tin. Prick the pastry base with a
fork. For large cases, cut a piece
of greaseproof paper rather
larger than the tin. Use this to
line the pastry and weight it
down with some dried beans,
pasta or rice.

Alternatively, crumple a piece
of foil and use that to line the
base of the pastry case. Bake the
pastry at the temperature given
in the recipe for 10–15 minutes,
then remove the baking beans
and paper, or the foil lining, and
return the tin to the oven for a
further 5 minutes to crisp the
pastry. Leave the baked case to
cool and shrink slightly before
removing it from the tin. (The
baking beans can be kept for use
again.)

For small cases, it is usually
sufficient to prick the pastry well
with a fork before baking.

Baked unfilled pastry cases
can be kept for a few days in an
airtight container.

INDEX